Praise

'*Get Your Career Unstuck* is for anyone who's ever woken up one morning and asked themselves, "Is this it?" Packed with practical tools and gentle nudges, this book will help you make real, sustainable life changes.'
— **Dr Sarah Quinn**, management consultant, international development

'*Get Your Career Unstuck* takes readers on a journey of self-discovery. It's filled with practical tips aimed at uncovering what's possible for genuine personal and career fulfilment. The humour sprinkled throughout the book, along with Roz's insights drawn from her experience, is complemented by science-backed facts and stories of inspiring people who have found success on their own terms. Together, these elements offer more than hope; they provide a solid foundation for those seeking meaningful change and a revitalised work life. Filled with actionable exercises designed to help you uncover your Fire Power, this book serves as a guide to reinvention, whether you're transitioning careers, facing downsizing or feeling that you have greater potential waiting to be unleashed. It also resonated with my own experience of finding passion doing something creative later in life as a trained business analyst. Reading this book is like discovering a beautifully crafted planner or stationery set – each page

filled with opportunities to design a life you love, reigniting your passion and setting you on a fresh new path.'
— **Carina Lawson**, founder, Ponderlily Paper & Planners

'With a background in founding businesses, navigating numerous career transitions and experiencing life across diverse cultures, I deeply understand the significance of aligning your vision and values with your professional path. In *Get Your Career Unstuck*, you'll discover practical exercises designed to unveil your genuine priorities, providing clarity and confidence as you pursue your career goals. If you find yourself feeling stuck in an unfulfilling job, this book equips you with the tools and insights needed to illuminate your path, guiding you towards a career journey that authentically reflects your essence and enhances your overall life satisfaction.'
— **Matthias Plunser**, entrepreneur, Selected Workspaces and the world's most remote co-working space

'In a world where career trajectories are anything but linear, *Get Your Career Unstuck* serves as a guiding light for the lost and the restless. With its empowering message and actionable advice, this book is a must-read for anyone embarking on the exhilarating journey of self-discovery and reinvention.'

— **Jenny Braithwaite**, founder, Magnify What You Do

'This book is an invaluable tool for anyone who's wanting to get unstuck and start their entrepreneurial journey. I wish I'd had this book ten years ago when I was feeling like something wasn't right in my career but I wasn't sure which way to go; I would have got here much quicker! *Get Your Career Unstuck* offers an effective combination of practical advice, frank talking, exercises to help you take action and inspirational case studies from people (just like you and me) who've made the leap themselves. This isn't a passive read – get ready to do the work, then reap the rewards.'

— **Pippa Goulden**, founder, The PR Set

GET YOUR CAREER

CAREER

DISCOVER YOUR INNER MAVERICK
AND TRANSFORM YOUR LIFE

UNSTUCK

Rozalyn Willocks

Re think

First published in Great Britain in 2024
by Rethink Press (www.rethinkpress.com)

To Mr Porter. You will be relieved to know I didn't go to prison; nor did I end up running the country.

Contents

Foreword

*G*et *Your Career Unstuck* is a beacon of hope for those feeling stuck in their professional lives. Offering practical and actionable advice, this book serves as a guiding light through the murky waters of frustration and uncertainty. Rozalyn provides relatable insights that resonate with readers, making the journey towards personal and professional fulfilment feel less daunting.

Each chapter is filled with tangible steps and strategies, empowering readers to take control of their career trajectories. What sets this book apart is its emphasis on unlocking one's true purpose. Rather than offering generic career advice, Rozalyn delves deep into the importance of aligning one's goals with one's passions and values. Through engaging anecdotes and exercises, readers are encouraged to explore their own motivations and aspirations, ultimately leading to a clearer sense of direction.

Whether you're a recent graduate struggling to find your footing or a seasoned professional seeking a change, you'll find that *Get Your Career Unstuck* offers invaluable guidance. Consider it your roadmap to a more fulfilling and purpose-driven career.

Paul Porter
Co-founder, Being Human at

Disclaimer

R eading this book may trigger moments of self-revelation and an irresistible impulse to overcome life's obstacles. Potential side effects might include a pervasive sense of purpose, an unyielding determination to pursue aspirations, and the realisation that your life could profoundly improve. Approach with levity and an open heart, as discovering your purpose ought to be accompanied by abundant joy! You hold the reins of your destiny.

The insights and actionable guidance within these pages have the power to transform the lives of countless individuals worldwide. However, they reflect one person's perspective. While they have proven effective for many and continue to do so, if you are unwilling to act, consider passing the book on to someone else. If, though – like me – you believe that, with proper guidance, there are few limits to what you can achieve, read on.

Before delving in, please note that any alterations to names or amalgamation of characters have been made to preserve anonymity. Despite my efforts to provide authoritative and precise information, I do not assume responsibility for your actions based on that information. I also do not accept liability for any outdated information, and the advice contained herein is timeless.

Introduction

'I want to work 60 hours per week, to buy a house which will take 30 years to pay off, so that I can retire and start living,' said no one, ever. However, that is precisely the path society conditions us to follow from an early age.

I bet you don't know the date you plan to retire. As reported in 2024 by *The Guardian*, the current retirement age is 66, but to sustain the ratio of workers per state pensioner, it will have to rise. This means that if you were born after 1970, you probably won't retire until you are 67. The predicted life expectancy is 72. Congratulations! You will have 5 years to enjoy your retirement; subject to good health, of course.

We have been programmed to believe that success equates to a big house, fast cars, influencer-style holidays and designer clothes. Somewhere along the way, we've lost our identity. Think back to your first dreams in life. At seven, perhaps you wanted to become an astronaut; as a teenager, you might have had plans to travel the world. It's likely, though, that you instead went to university, got a job, bought a house and got into debt. Maybe you married and had kids. Perhaps you now busy yourself with meetings, fitness classes and ferrying your children around, all the while working hard so you could afford life's essentials and two weeks of holiday each year in the sun. It's likely you are still thinking, 'One day…' No wonder so many people succumb to midlife crises.

You know that feeling of being stuck that you are experiencing? That nagging feeling that there is more to life? That you don't really fit in, but you can't put your finger on why? It's likely that this sense of being stuck – of feeling trapped and unfulfilled in an otherwise successful career – hits you around midlife, although it can start earlier. That feeling isn't going away. I know – I've been there.

We have been mis-sold a dream – conditioned to believe that the harder we work, the luckier and more successful we will be. The stories in this book will show you that success is not based on working harder and longer hours. Success comes from:

- Leveraging fear

- Taking calculated risks

- Knowing your destination and, importantly, your purpose of why you are working towards that destination

I'm going to take you on a journey to help you get unstuck, one action at a time. It's a journey you can take at any age and at any point on your career ladder. It's also a journey I've taken myself, and thanks to the knowledge I have gathered in 20 years of working in recruitment, I help my coaching clients do the same.

It took me until I was in my thirties and experiencing my first career change to work out that my feelings of not fitting in at work and of being stuck were largely down to my values. It was only when I became self-employed that I started to really thrive. I was able to pick the clients and the projects I wanted to work on. No longer did I have to attend meaningless meetings, wade through bureaucracy or report to someone less qualified than me.

My new work – picking up various contracting gigs for corporates working in the recruitment space – was much more fulfilling. I was advising founders of small- to medium-sized enterprises (SMEs) and startups on how to attract candidates, and on how to develop their recruitment process as they started to scale. I also enjoyed giving candidates feedback, coaching them on their interview techniques, and helping them improve their CVs and LinkedIn profiles. I was motivated by the messages I received from people who thanked me and described how my feedback had helped them secure new work positions. Friends and colleagues who felt unfulfilled started to tap me up for career advice, and before long, I found myself coaching and mentoring referrals.

As a career strategist and mentor, I've developed a straightforward approach to assist men and women in overcoming challenges and navigating career transitions, whether those are through choice or due to circumstances such as redundancy. This approach guides individuals through the stages of feeling stuck, overwhelmed and fearful. It helps people to recognise their own Fire Power, explore opportunities for the next steps in their careers, and take action. Fire Power is the effective power or force you have, and your skills, influence and potential for action and achieving results.

Everyone deserves to live a life less ordinary, after all, we are creators, the architects of our lives. Life should be a double scoop of raspberry ripple and biscotti, with hundreds and thousands and plenty of chocolate flakes on top. It should be purposeful, intentional and vibrant. We all have infinite potential to live a more meaningful life. It shouldn't be about sitting in some mundane, soul-sucking job, going through the motions, while chasing society's promise that one day you can retire and start living. That is an illusion. Following your dreams is the ultimate blueprint for satisfaction.

In *Get Your Career Unstuck* I have included anecdotes and coaching exercises to help you get unstuck. I will help you imagine your future in detail, whether you are seeking new challenges, retraining to move into a new field, or growing a business from a side hustle or personal passion. I will walk you through how to identify and maximise your transferable skills, especially your superpowers – your Fire Power. Then you'll be operating in your genius zone – the area where you can offer something unique from your authentic self. You'll be in a flow state, completely absorbed in what you are doing, so work will seem effortless.

I have also included stories from inspiring people who found success after getting unstuck, by following their dreams and the unconventional path. I have intentionally not added tales from anyone claiming to have quit their job and become an overnight success, earning six or seven figures and jet-setting around the globe, because those stories aren't real. Instead, I have selected authentic people who have quit the rat race to live life on their terms, because I want to show you it can be done. I refer to these people as 'Mavericks'. They are from all walks of life and have in common that they have dared to take a leap and follow their heart. Their stories, in the form of letters, will inspire you along your journey through this book. I want to help you become one of them.

Reading this book is not mandatory; you can put it down and continue on your current path, or you can buckle up and commit to taking action. Planning and working towards your escape from the rat race is a bit like eating an elephant: it's best done one chunk at a time. I mean this metaphorically, of course; please don't endeavour to eat an elephant, unless it's made of chocolate (yum).

May this book be your blueprint for success, fuelled by your Fire Power. Welcome to mission *Get Your Career Unstuck*. It's time to level up your life.

PART ONE
STUCK IN THE MUD

ONE
Take Stock

If you live to the age of 72, you will have about 26,298 days on this planet. When I think about my days being numbered, I appreciate the importance of making each one count. What have you done today that's got you fired up, excited and bursting with joy? If you are hard-pressed to think of something, rest assured that you are not alone.

Most people go through education to get a good job and to buy a house. Most people then end up fighting through a long and expensive commute, peppered with delays, and racing to their corporate cubicles by 8.30am to attend pointless meetings, jump through bureaucratic hoops and work long hours. All this to get promoted, so they can afford to go on holiday to escape the endless monotony of work, while they dream of retiring so they can start living. There is a reason it is called 'earning a living'. Somewhere in between all that, they reward themselves with nights out, shopping sprees and holidays they can't really afford.

If that is similar to your own situation, the danger is that ten years from now, you will almost certainly still be doing the same thing. You can all too easily get stuck in a loop, in groundhog day, going nowhere. You won't find judgement from me on this – I have been there. The rat race boils down to an exhausting weekly cycle of work to benefit shareholders, where you exchange your time for limited monetary compensation. The idea that having, doing and being 'more' is the key to happiness is a perpetual state of unawareness. Momentarily, you lift your head above the parapet, yearning for something else, but you don't know how to make the leap.

In my thirties, my godmother passed away unexpectedly from heart failure. She had been looking forward to semi-retirement and shared with me her excitement about rediscovering hobbies such as horseriding and art, and the fact that she'd decided to embark on a course in holistic therapy. We were making plans for her to visit me in the UK. She was my closet confidante and, at the time, my biggest cheerleader. Her zest for life was infectious. Her tragic passing pulled the rug from beneath me. It was so final and felt unfair. She had worked hard and finally had time to follow her passions and spend time with the people she loved. I was petrified that I'd reach 70 years of age still not retired, doing the daily grind and living a life less ordinary, and not feeling proud of what I had achieved. Worse still, I worried I would die before I'd completed my bucket list. I had images of my tombstone bearing the words *She led an ordinary life*. Bronnie Ware is a palliative care nurse. In her article 'Regrets of the dying', she writes that the number one regret when dying is, unsurprisingly, 'I wish I'd had the courage to live a life true to myself, not the life others expected of me.' If that's not enough to motivate you into action, I don't know what is.

Slapped by a wet kipper

What's your bucket list? You know – if you could quit right now, go anywhere, be whoever you wanted and do whatever you wanted, what would you do? We yearn for change but don't always know where to begin or how to get there. We know that we are not content. We have a dream, but it feels out of reach. We don't know where to begin and procrastinate for fear of the unknown. We end up in a state of analysis paralysis, sticking our heads in the sand. Or we escape by busying ourselves with errands, acquiring more qualifications, buying things – all to distract us from being present and facing up to that little voice willing us to act. Generally, we stay in our uncomfortable comfort zone because change is even more unsettling. Until you become self-aware and learn how to live more consciously, rather you will continue going through the motions on autopilot.

Our lizard brain, which governs our survival instincts, has taken over. It is keeping us safe from failure by telling us we are not worthy or deserving of success, or that we can't afford to take the necessary action. Sometimes, it even makes us fearful of being visible. The thing about fear, though, is that it blocks action. After all, we are designed to steer away from a perceived threat. Our fight, flight, freeze or fawn mode kicks in, trying to keep us safe, but that keeps us small. Don't busy yourself drowning out those fears with Netflix, booze, food and shopping – the fears will only grow louder. Instead, listen to them. Rationalise them.

It is usually around middle age when the sobering realisation of this sets in. Perhaps it is because we are halfway through our 26,298 days. Maybe it is because, around this time, we have to think seriously about retirement and pension planning – something many of us have ignored. It may also be because ageing relatives have passed on, making us start to think about later life through a much closer lens. That inner voice gets louder – it's now more like a Mariachi band – and usually manifests itself in depression, redundancy, illness, relationship breakdowns or some other life event, which slaps us across the face like a wet kipper.

I call this the *midlife maverick wakeup call*. It is usually around this time that coaching clients contact me. They are stuck in a quagmire and can't see a way out.

I have noticed clients in their thirties are also starting to hear their inner voice, which I suspect is due to the impact of lockdown on people's mental health. People had more time to think. They also felt more vulnerable. They realised that a lot of the things that seemed important weren't. They found themselves asking: *Is this really it?*

According to a 2015 survey by the London School of Business and Finance, nearly half of all workers in the UK (47%) admit they do not find their jobs fulfilling and say they would like to change careers. Unsurprisingly, a 2015 study by Gallup found those who get to do what they want to do every day are six times as likely to be engaged and to report having an excellent quality of life.

How are you, really?

Let's be frank: most people today feel overworked, underpaid, overwhelmed, underdeveloped and undervalued. Just about everyone craves purpose, challenge, autonomy, creativity and collaboration with inspiring people. Instead, people find themselves working in lousy offices, commuting unnecessarily to meaningless meetings, being micromanaged and working long hours on projects that often get scrapped. They probably also have crappy bosses giving them lip service and zero support.

In its report *Employee Burnout: Causes and cures*, Gallup found the biggest causes of burnout, in order, to be:

- Unfair treatment at work

- Unclear communication from managers

- Unmanageable workload

- Lack of manager support

- Unreasonable time pressure

No wonder people are feeling disengaged. Cue the new trend of employees quietly quitting or cybersurfing for other jobs, or 'career cushioning' – looking for new work as a plan B for potential redundancy.

'Work is no longer simply about the pay cheque,' says Gian Power, Founder of TLC Lions, which assists large corporations with inclusion, mental health and talent development. 'Professional success for many is now about finding happiness in their life,' he says. 'I've had friends quit their corporate jobs without a next job lined up. Why? Because they can't take it anymore. They are not inspired by their leaders, and they don't aspire to be at the top if it means only financial gain and a real loss of happiness.'

It's time to ask yourself, *How did I get here?* And more importantly, *What am I going to do about it?* Life is too short for ordinary. If you're getting that Sunday sinking feeling, or if you find yourself clock-watching, willing the working day to end, then it's time to act and start working on your escape plan. That was certainly the case for Dean Nicholson, a welder from Scotland. According to the BBC article 'The cat who hitched a lift on a worldwide tour', Dean, sick of his nine-to-five existence, decided to get on his bike and see the world. He's amassed millions of followers on social media, who follow his adventures through Europe – now in a van – with his sidekick, Nala the cat.

How did we get here? If you're a Gen Xer, it's likely you are sandwiched between those smug baby boomers with their stable careers, comfy pensions and no mortgages; and those millennials, who love to challenge your 'just do it' work ethic.

Generation X has a whole different take on the working world, which really makes sense. We grew up rebelling against the status quo, craving more excitement in our careers and lives than our parents ever did. We opened doors to having it all but not in the way the baby boomers did, with their booming economies, affordable homes, job security, one-income households and lifelong employment, before they quit work by the age of 55, still with enough gas in the tank to enjoy retirement.

Gen Xers are juggling double incomes to pay for everything, from school expenses like stationery, uniforms and lunches, to childcare and mortgages, while competing with a global workforce. No wonder our career values have done a 180. While our parents believed in sticking with one company for life, we rebelled against that and job hopped to boost our salaries. We transformed our workplaces into hubs for temporary positions, working across borders, showing our love for dynamic change. Non-linear careers are becoming the norm, with the focus shifting towards lifelong learning rather than lifetime loyalty to one company or path. According to the Phoenix Insights report *Careers Advice For Longer Lives*, a third of 45- to 54-year-olds expect to change career before retirement.

Despite all the tech wizardry around us, our commute times and work hours seem to stretch on forever. For many of us, work isn't just about paying bills; it's a big part of who we are. We can't leave our careers to chance, and lots of us – in our forties or fifties – are questioning if we can keep this pace up. Unlike our parents, we'll probably work well into our eighties. Retirement as we know it might be a distant dream.

What do you want?

Of course, if you knew that, you wouldn't be here, right? I hear you. OK, let's start with easier questions:

- What motivated you to pick up this book?

- What impact is 'being stuck' having on you?

- Why do you want a career change?

- What don't you want?

- What is no longer serving you?

- Where is your energy gauge right now?

- What brings you joy and makes you happy?

- Which people in your life energise you?

- Which places energise you?

Now think about what drains you. As you do that, recognise your emotions and how your energy changes. I used to have a manager who would show up to meetings on a Friday and spend 45 minutes talking over me. It wasn't a collaborative meeting, and there was no innovative thinking – it was just her downloading. I would come away feeling drained and demoralised. I would contemplate this over and over, thinking about how I resented being trapped in a job because it paid well and allowed me to afford my hefty mortgage. I was on the way to burnout, again.

Stop solving and start listening

If you spend your time in solution mode, problem solving, writing lists and coming up with plans...

STOP. You need to get out of head mode and into heart mode. It's easier said than done, but the following exercise will help.

EXERCISE: Following your heart

Find a quiet place where you won't be interrupted. I know that can be tricky if you have kids and pets, but the bathroom or a shed can be a good place to escape to.

Be still, not focusing on the gardening, washing up, TV or running errands. Just be.

Take three deep breaths.

Ask yourself, What is no longer bringing me joy?

Give yourself permission to sit with this, no matter how uncomfortable it might be. Really reflect on what resistance is there. Where is the tension? Is it in your neck, shoulders, back, head, throat, heart?

Audit your energy. Notice what emotions are coming up for you. Feelings of sadness, regret, frustration, loneliness, anger, anxiety, overwhelm, despair and inadequacy are all normal. You might want to cry, scream, shout or just lie down and just be still – this is your body's way of getting rid of energy blockages.

Whatever comes up for you in that exercise, sit with it. Be present. Allow yourself to experience the emotions. Often, we are too quick to dismiss them. We drown them out, bottle them up and quickly busy ourselves with errands. That's not healthy, and the emotions will eventually manifest into physical symptoms – stress, anxiety, panic attacks, depression or disease.

Acknowledging the emotions coming up for you is a vital part of self-care and allows you to heal. Think of these emotions as that inner voice knocking on the door of your conscious mind, sending a signal and saying, *Hey, you deserve more.* By listening to your emotions and honouring them, you are soothing your sympathetic nervous system. As caretaker, you are reassuring your body, mind and soul that you are taking action.

After that exercise, place your hands on your heart and take the opportunity to thank your body for bringing the emotions to the forefront. You may feel drained, so I encourage you to ground yourself – not with chocolate or a large glass of wine, but by being in nature. Walk around the garden barefooted, hug a tree or make yourself a herbal tea and put on some sooth-ing music. Give yourself permission to relax and be still. When we feel fulfilled, we are in flow, energised and tapped into our life force, and we feel optimised. We have clarity, alignment and a sense of peace. When we're unfulfilled, we are blocked and feel restless. The illustration below gives examples of the emotions we feel in our different energy zones.

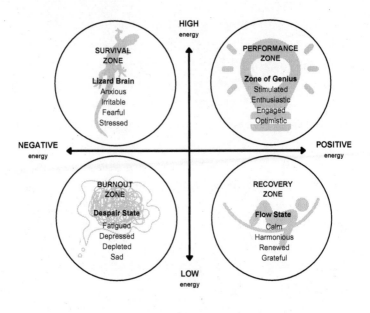

EXERCISE: Job satisfaction wheel

Once you are feeling grounded, draw a job satisfaction wheel on a piece of paper, using the illustration below as a guide. Especially if you haven't felt creative for a while, I encourage you to really enjoy this process. You may want to use different-coloured pens, card and paper. Be as creative as you like – there is no right or wrong way of doing this exercise.

Draw a circle and, like a pie chart, divide it into eight segments:

1. Pay and benefits
2. Job security
3. Opportunities to use skills
4. Safety of work environment

5. Relationships with colleagues
6. Relationships with management
7. Fun at work
8. Meaningful work

Add the numbers 1 to 10 along each segment, with 1 representing unsatisfied and 10 representing fully satisfied.

Shade in each segment to represent how you feel about it right now.

Now step back and review the job satisfaction wheel. Notice the areas that you have shaded as unsatisfied. Don't panic if most of the wheel is shaded as unsatisfied – having a visual representation is a helpful starting point to recognise the areas that are most lacking and in need of attention. Sometimes, you won't necessarily know why you feel unfulfilled in your job – it can be due to multiple reasons.

I find this exercise useful to reflect on the different areas and see what comes up for me. All facets are important.

Look at the sections that you have shaded 5 and below. Can some of these areas be addressed without moving jobs? Perhaps you have a desire to upskill and would welcome a secondment. Perhaps requesting flexible working would give you more work–life balance. Is reducing the number of days you work a financial option?

Pin the completed job satisfaction wheel on your wall or fridge and review it over the next weeks and months to mark any changes in your levels of satisfaction. I like to revisit the wheel and shade in a different colour so I can visually see changes.

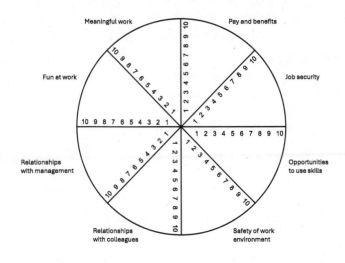

What works, and what doesn't?

Before you can define the life and career you want, sometimes the starting point is recognising what *isn't* working. It's important to be honest about where you are, and to get in touch with who you are and how you want to show up.

When we are in survival mode, we often stay at the surface of our emotions because we don't want to tap into how sad we are feeling. Making a change also often feels like a big leap. Having a North Star to work towards is exciting, but sometimes we latch on to an idea that is short-lived because we have not taken time to really understand what we want or need.

I encourage you to be open-minded and explore any opportunities that come along. Allow yourself to experiment and allow the journey to bend, weave, unfold and evolve (sounds like a Hallmark card, but go with me on this). This is all part of your new learning experience in finding out what *does* work. The final destination is the grave, so make the journey count.

To truly become unstuck, you need to delve deeper, embrace the uncomfortable and give yourself permission to process feelings. Don't approach this part of the process as a chore that needs ticking off the list before you quickly move onto the next item – you would be doing yourself an injustice.

The stuck-in-the-mud questions

Ask yourself the powerful questions outlined below to gain a deeper understanding of yourself, your passions and your purpose. Armed with this self-awareness, you can make more informed decisions about your career choices and the lifestyle you want. You are only one choice away from a different life. It's time to stop being the passenger and be in the driving seat instead.

The best results come from not rushing through the questions. Instead, ruminate on what each question is asking and what that means to you, noticing the feelings it stimulates.

EXERCISE: Stuck-in-the-mud questions

You may want to write the questions out and list your answers; or draw a mind map, with bubbles branching off to the answers that come up. Many of my clients find this exercise eye-opening.

The questions are designed to challenge you and give you clarity on where you are and what matters to you. Be honest with yourself.

- If I choose to continue on my current path, where will I be in 1 year, 5 years, 10 years or 20 years from now?
- What's the price I am paying for staying stuck in my current situation?
- What is the story I have been telling myself about my current situation? Is that story empowering or disempowering me?
- What is making me self-sabotage my ability to move forward?
- What else is holding me back?
- What is my fear telling me?
- Why am I feeling this way? Does my own behaviour or attitude contribute to this?
- What does success look like for me? How would it feel?

- What legacy do I want to leave behind in my career and life? How can I start building that legacy today?
- If I could speak to my role model or someone I admire for five minutes, what would I ask them?
- What are the most common distractions and time-wasting activities in my life? How could I eliminate or minimise them?
- On my deathbed, what advice would I give to my younger self?
- How do I want to show up? How would I like the world to see me?
- What if I did the opposite of what I am doing now? How might that change my outcomes?
- If I could only work two hours per week on my business, what would I focus on to achieve the most significant results?
- If I had to teach someone everything I know in just 30 minutes, what key concepts would I cover?
- What activities or commitments in my life no longer serve my goals or happiness? How can I let go of them?
- What's the difference between what I want and what I am currently settling for? How can I close that gap?
- What could the reward be for taking massive action?
- If not now, when will I make this change?

Summary

You have to start from where you are on this journey, with an honest appraisal of your current situation and level of energy. Chapter One has provided resources to help you achieve this. The stuck-in-the-mud questions in the final exercise above will give you clarity and help you to make informed choices on what you need to change and why.

The Maverick Letters

These are the first two letters from Mavericks who have made the leap. You will find other letters at the end of the other chapters.

Josh Heyneke, Parc Carreg Farm

To all you dreamers

I am an entrepreneur and a regenerative farmer, living in Wales. I haven't always been a farmer, and neither my parents nor my grandparents were farmers. I grew up in the city of Cape Town, South Africa, with access to beautiful outdoor spaces. Little did I know how much impact these green spaces would have on my career. There was no clear path for me to become a farmer, and I didn't even know I wanted to be one until much later in life.

In 2009 I had finished studying marketing and recently got married to the love of my life, Abigail. We found ourselves in London looking for jobs. The economy was a wreck, and most companies were firing, not hiring. Eventually, I found an unpaid internship, working as a sales assistant for a small startup company that built mobile apps. Computers and technology were a passion of mine, so this opportunity was perfect and led to what I considered to be my dream job, working with people I liked, doing interesting projects.

However, after seven years living and working in London, I started to feel the impact on my physical and mental health. I spent a lot of time in the office behind a computer. I became unfit. My childhood asthma came back, and I started suffering from anxiety. Something wasn't quite right. I felt unfulfilled. The career path ahead was clear to me, but it was no longer exciting. Something had changed. I was desperate to take on a new challenge.

The seed of radical change was sown when I started experimenting with my diet as a way to help improve my health. I remember reading a study comparing the nutritional value of a vegetable that had been freshly picked with one that was stored on a supermarket shelf. Abigail and I had to start growing our own food. This led us both onto permaculture, and down the rabbit hole we went. It wasn't long before we came across the concept of regenerative agriculture – the idea that we could produce healthy food while having a positive impact on the environment.

We had often joked about buying a farm when we retired. We started thinking very seriously about what we wanted from our lives. Suddenly, the urge to break free from city life and start an alternate life in the countryside became overwhelming. We realised that if we really wanted to farm, we should start young rather than waiting until we're old. Life is too short. We wanted to work outside in the fresh air – rain or shine – and we wanted to get our hands dirty.

How would we afford to buy a farm, though? We had a vague plan, but the path ahead was unclear. In 2015 we decided to quit our jobs, sell our flat in London and disappear into the countryside in search of some land. I look back today, and I still can't believe how crazy we were to make this decision. We weren't exactly ignorant to the risk involved, so we must have been a bit drunk with optimism.

Since then, we've been on the adventure of our lives. We built a beautiful regenerative farm, experimented with a lot of different ideas and eventually became known as the UK's only organic duck egg producer – crazy. It's been an incredibly rewarding but also a challenging period of our lives. In fact, it's been so tough that I don't think our older selves would have pursued this venture if we had known the challenges we would face. We put every penny of our savings and every moment of our time into the farm. We hadn't taken a single holiday in seven years. Our customers loved our eggs and the way we raised our ducks. We made our way onto multiple television and radio programmes and podcasts.

At the same time, the egg industry was facing enormous challenges, and we narrowly escaped bankruptcy in 2022. Little did we know that March 2023 would be far worse. In the process of trying to export fertilised hatching eggs to a customer in Europe, who wanted our breed of ducks, we discovered through testing that our flock was carrying salmonella, despite being in good health. We learned the hard way that raising free range, organic, unvaccinated ducks comes with its risks. We were forced by the Food Standards Authority to stop selling eggs until we had 'depopulated' and replaced our flock. It was at this point that we realised we needed to make another change. We decided to stop producing organic duck eggs – we had sacrificed too much already. I don't think I could imagine a worse ending for the farm business – we were distraught and exhausted.

Now, though, we haven't been so happy in a long time. Since we started our farming in 2015, regenerative agriculture has become a hot topic. Since closing the egg business, we have been approached by a few companies who are interested in the regenerative methodologies and practices that we developed with our ducks on Parc Carreg. We are now consulting on other regenerative farm projects while continuing to experiment with and develop new ideas on our own farm. We still keep ducks, and we have so much more that we plan to do. We've found our second wind and are ready for the next seven years in agriculture.

What can you – a fellow dreamer – take away from this? Well, sometimes dreams don't work out the way you want them to, but that does not mean you shouldn't pursue them. Even though we failed to achieve exactly what we had set out to do, and things ended really badly, those seven years of hard work and heartache have turned into a real asset, which has led us on to the next chapter of our lives. We often get asked if we would do anything differently, and the honest answer is no. We needed each and every single one of our experiences to be where we are today. Life is a series of stepping stones. Go ahead and follow your heart, scratch that itch, be prepared to fail, go with the flow and enjoy the rollercoaster ride.

Josh and Abi
www.parccarreg.com

André Gagiano, Strike North

Dear Commuter,

Have you ever dreamed of leaving your cubicle career behind and freeing yourself from the daily grind? Swapping out the daily commute for something a little more exotic? The jump is scary. In an earlier life, I often looked at those giving up corporate life and diving into something else as irresponsible, even childish. The nine-to-five has become a symbol of being a grown-up. We leave our dreams at the office door and pick them up when we catch a glimpse of an exotic photo. They are usually reserved for gap years or when booking our once-a-year holidays.

It doesn't have to be like this. I too had a daily commute – Bakerloo line, changing onto the Piccadilly, and then a mad dash to the office, smoke in one hand, Metro in the other. I spent 20-plus years working in commodities, starting with an internship in London. It was hard-paced, exciting, and the rewards were enough to keep any other dreams I had at bay.

I ended up working in West Africa. My dream of having a family was slowly fading away. By some amazing luck and a friend's wedding, I finally ended up tying the knot and starting a family of my own. What was the deciding factor for me leaving my career? It started with me finally having the family I always dreamed of and not wanting to spend time away from my wife and kids. With my focus shifting, giving my all to both work and family became a struggle.

To add to the mix, my youngest battled malaria twice before turning one, and then there was an Ebola scare in the country. Anxiety hit the roof. My wife and I decided it was time to pack our bags and head back to Europe, but my time away from the family triggered massive guilt. Childhood anxieties, long forgotten, resurfaced. The more I distanced myself from them, the more frustrated I became. Having made two investments that needed more focus, I made the jump. Unfortunately, they didn't work out.

I've wrestled with various roles since, trying to find my place. From immersing myself in graphic design to crafting brand strategy and steering as a project manager for a tech company, these ventures stand in stark contrast to my previous life in commodities. There I engaged in everything from finance and operations to management.

I've finally found my niche. I am a co-owner of a surf rental shop in Portugal, consultant for startups and life coach catering to 40- to 50-year-olds looking to jump from corporate into something more meaningful.

Portugal has the perfect mix of both Europe and what reminds me of Africa. The climate is very similar to my childhood growing up in Cape Town. My kids are trilingual. I've rekindled my relationship with surfing after a 20-year hiatus. I spend a lot more time with my wife and kids. Life has become slower in many respects. I feel a deeper sense of connection with my family. I savour the time I have with my kids. I'm acutely aware that this time I have with them is limited, and that I don't get to put life on hold until everything is perfect. My kids grow every day. The gig economy has been good to me, but it has taken me a while to figure it all out.

What would I do differently, with hindsight? What do I want to do? What can I be paid to do? What narrative is running through my life story?

You'll need to ask yourself the same questions. What is consistently showing up? What hard and soft skills have you picked up over your career? What values are you lined up with, and are you living within these? This will give you the foundation with which to work. Get an idea of what you can be paid for and turn it into a side hustle. Yeah – that awful expression made popular by influencers sitting in Bali next to exotic cars. Hear me out. This is where you test it out, while you still have your pay cheque. Does it work? How would it fit into the life you want?

Where do you want to live? Is it the weather you are looking for? Maybe it's outdoor activities? Two weeks away with powder conditions or solid six-foot barrels is not a realistic benchmark. Travel to the places you think you want to live in the off-season. Recce it. Do you have kids? What are schools like? Is there an airport nearby? Tap into the local community.

Do I regret my decision in leaving the normal nine-to-five behind? It's been challenging at times. Frustrating, lonely and scary. I've tapped into something that feels deeper, though. I feel more in tune with my family and myself. Things that used to bother me beforehand no longer have any power over me. I view the world very differently than before.

The irony is that when you're working up the well-paid ladder, it seems there is never enough money. Stress is high, and it feels as if you are endlessly working towards something that continues to remain elusive. Maybe because it is.

When have you sat down and truly thought about where you are at and what makes you tick?

With some careful planning and consideration, moving yourself out of the rat race is easier than you might think.

See you on the other side.

André
www.strikenorth.com

TWO

Embrace Your Fear

I 'm not going to sugar-coat this. Let's be frank: the biggest obstacle is you. Ask yourself: *How am I getting in my own way? Why am I holding myself back?*

The answers often come down to fear, which is a self-imposed limitation. Ask yourself where this fear has come from.

In his TEDx talk about 'Quieting the lizard brain', Seth Godin talks about our lizard brain being the biggest gatekeeper to acting and making change. What's getting in the way of you following your dreams? What do you need to change in your life to achieve all that you can? Often, when we are stuck and fearful of trying something new, it is because we fear the unknown. We talk ourselves out of taking action.

Here are just a few examples of the fears that might be holding you back:

- Fear of being visible because you don't want to be humiliated and worry what others think of you

- Fear of failing

- Fear of being successful

- Fear of not being able to financially support yourself

- Fear of not being good enough and feeling inadequate

- Fear of not 'making it' before you die

A vital success factor is discarding the fears that do not serve us and which hinder our success and happiness. Your comfort zone can be a cosy place but it stifles dreams. The illustration below shows the benefits of stepping out of your comfort zone.

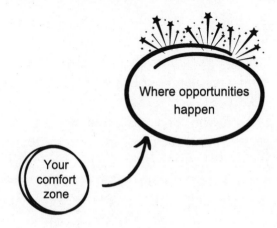

Where opportunities happen

Your comfort zone

We talk ourselves out of trying new things until we feel financially secure, lose weight, buy a house, find a relationship, get that promotion. All the time, life is passing by, and we risk being in the same place 12 months from now.

What if you reframed the fear?

What if you changed your perspective, took action, put yourself out there, and saw failure as a way to grow, innovate and move forward?

Failure can be a positive thing. It brings new learning, self-awareness, opportunities, skills and new people into our lives, all of which is rewarding. Remind yourself that fear and failures are OK – it is where the magic happens. Think of Edison inventing the light-bulb, when he said, 'I've not failed. I've just found 10,000 ways that won't work.' In his article 'How to cultivate a growth mindset', Tony Robbins states, 'If you are not growing, you are dying.' Don't wait until you have it all figured out. There is no such thing as the right time.

Facing your frog

It's not our fault, of course. Many of our fears stem from the influence of our ego – the aspect of us that is fixated on gaining recognition and avoiding ostracism. It's your Larry Lounge Lizard ego (anyone remember him from the 1980s?). Initiating and effecting change requires you to confront and release your ego, which can feel a challenging endeavour, given its longstanding influence. Over your lifetime, your ego has held you back, and it isn't likely to exit quietly. Instead, it may attempt to sabotage your well-intentioned plans by sowing seeds of self-doubt, and instilling fears of financial ruin, criticism, shame, humiliation and isolation. While your ego strives to keep you safe, it also keeps you in your comfort zone, playing small. Taking decisive action is the key to disrupting this pattern.

Shirzad Chamine, a Stanford University lecturer and advocate for positive intelligence, asserts in his 2013 TED Talk that each of us harbours inner saboteurs. Our saboteurs can vary in their influence, with some exerting louder voices than others. They originate from the primal, survival-orientated region of the brain, while our sage represents the positive-intelligence aspect. The survival-orientated part of the brain is inherently wired to experience stress and discontent. To attain sustained happiness, Chamine suggests we must reinforce our positive intelligence.

My inner ego has held me back, preventing me from participating in speaking events, attending special occasions and taking incredible opportunities. It can be debilitating. My ego sits on my shoulder, filling me with self-doubt. To disempower him, I have given him a persona. I imagine him looking like Kermit the Frog from the Muppets, and I've named him Froggy.

When he speaks, I imagine his comical voice, which makes me smile, and the fear fades. I've learned to express gratitude to Froggy for his concern, reassuring him gently that he doesn't need to worry, that I am safe and that I can handle the situation. He soon fades away. Facing your frog can be liberating. It just takes a little time until the voice on your shoulder gets smaller, while you get braver.

When we experience success, love, money and creativity, it is not unusual for us to self-sabotage. We fall back into our familiar state of playing small, and feeling safe and comfortable. When something positive has happened, like receiving a bonus, how many times you have rushed home to tell your spouse, excited to share your news, but for some reason, the evening has ended up in a row?

Gay Hendricks talks about this in his book *The Big Leap*. He refers to it as the Upper Limit. Perhaps you achieved a gold star and ran home to tell your parents, who were too busy with work or caring for your younger sibling to celebrate your efforts. Over time, you learn to downplay your achievements to fit in and toe the line. You learn to blend in instead of speaking up. In adulthood, you are then uncomfortable receiving recognition – you dismiss compliments. Your Upper Limit holds you back, keeps you small and self-conscious, and prevents you from putting yourself forward to further your career.

Think back to times when you have been successful in something and a drama has ensued. Think about the events that led up to that moment – the change in energy. What happened that prevented you from enjoying your enhanced success – perhaps ill health, money woes or a relationship conflict? We often put failure down to bad luck or tell ourselves the universe is against us, but the reality is we have self-sabotaged the situation to keep us safe in our comfort zone. You may meet a new partner who is great and all's going well. Then your ego's voice creeps in (that damn frog), telling you that you don't deserve to be happy, so you find an excuse to end the relationship. Ask yourself what is behind the critique. Befriend it. Gently turn your frog down. Thank it, tell it you don't need help this time, but that when you do, you will ask for it.

Limiting beliefs

When I was in my twenties, I dreamed of owning my own business. I had so many ideas and wrote lots of business plans but then never executed them. Some of those ventures had the potential to be successful, but doubt set in, and I found a reason why it wouldn't work.

After I finished university, I took on a temping job at an office surrounded by other offices. There wasn't a sandwich shop anywhere nearby. I watched the office workers live off Pot Noodles, instant soups and food from the vending machine. I then got busy sketching out a plan for a sandwich business.

I decided I would employ local mothers who needed extra income with flexible hours, to work around school drop-off and pick-up times. I planned to make up baskets of sandwiches and snacks, and have the mothers go around the offices selling them. In 2001 few companies had onsite catering. Pret a Manger and Starbucks existed, but only in city centres.

Despite the viability of my plans, fear crept in:

- Where would I get the finance?
- What if I failed?
- What if I ended up in debt?
- What if I couldn't find staff?
- Where would I find premises to make the sandwiches?

I talked myself out of proceeding with the venture.

Months later, a friend proposed a mobile massage business, providing shoulder massages to office workers. Again, in the early 2000s, this type of business model was relatively unheard of. Staff wellbeing programmes didn't exist. Guess what, though – I talked myself out of it again:

- What if we didn't make any sales?

- What if the business was a flop, and I would be a laughing stock?

- What if I bumped into my arch enemy from school?

I even asked myself, *What if the business is a success and delays my plans to move to London?* Of course, I look back now and kick myself. Even if either of these businesses had failed, imagine the learning experience, the adventures along the way, the memories, the people I would have met and the mentors I would have learned from. If the ventures had failed, I could also have returned to temping.

When we play small, it is because we feel flawed in some way – like something is wrong with us, that we are not deserving of success. We convince ourselves we don't have the support, the knowledge, skill, time or resources others do, and that somehow our idea, product or service is inferior. How many times have you looked at colleagues, friends and people in the media and told yourself that they succeeded because they are smarter, more beautiful, skinnier, talented, better educated, come from wealth or have supportive families? While I don't dispute there are people who have been born with silver spoons in their mouths, there are far more people who have come from nothing and still succeed.

MONEY MINDSET MATTERS

I had a friend called Paul. Paul was nearly 50 and a talented hairdresser, but he had a negative relationship with money. He had divorced twice and saw his kids on his days off. He rented a two-bed flat and had sold his car to get by. He would complain endlessly about not having enough money.

When I asked Paul what he thought was within his control, he stopped in his tracks. I could see he hadn't thought about this before, and the cogs were working hard. He eventually shrugged his shoulders and changed the topic.

Later that evening, I sent Paul a blog post called 'How limiting beliefs are keeping you broke', in which the author talks about money as energy. When we consistently make statements about not having enough or being broke, we are wiring our brains from a place of lack rather than abundance. Paul was wiring his brain to believe he wasn't deserving of money. He was self-sabotaging and repelling money rather than attracting it.

His fear of not having enough and being broke was self-perpetuating. Each time Paul got paid, something would go wrong. His son broke his tooth playing football and needed dental care; the water pipe in the salon burst forcing him to close his business temporarily; his landlady was putting the rent up. Paul also complained about not seeing his teenage daughter, saying she only contacted him when she needed money. His daughter had adopted Paul's scarcity mindset about money.

The next time I visited Paul, he was upbeat, cheerful and more relaxed. He introduced me to his daughter, who he'd recently hired as a Saturday assistant. He'd negotiated a deal with his landlady so she would forego putting up the rent in exchange for him helping out with handyman jobs. He'd also realised that renting a two-bedroom flat wasn't necessary and was looking for a one-bed.

By changing his mindset, Paul had improved his financial situation. He was also getting to spend more time with his daughter, and she was earning money working at the salon.

Rejection – the fear of being excluded or judged by your family, friends and colleagues – may be another thing that has held you back. Perhaps you didn't embark on your chosen career for fear of not meeting your parents' expectations. You may find when you talk about a career change, you are met with silence; or, worse still, stories about Great-Aunt Phyllis and Great-Uncle Bert ploughing their life savings into a bakery business that failed. Perhaps your colleagues cannot understand why you would want to abandon a prestigious job role to pursue a writing career. They voice their concerns about the instability of freelancing and the financial risk. Your peers may even undermine your confidence by questioning your talent. Their caution may be born out of jealousy and fear that your success may highlight their own dissatisfaction with their career. Sometimes, friends can express resistance because they worry your career change will disrupt the social circle or create distance between you and them. Sadly, they may even belittle your ideas as unrealistic, which can be disheartening.

My friend Sarah has the opposite situation with her family. They are fearless and have an incredibly positive mindset, open to possibility. Sarah's parents are unconditionally supportive of their three children and brought them up to believe they could achieve anything. As a result, Sarah is one of the most confident and determined individuals I have met. She knew if she failed at something she would have her family's support, no matter what. Imagine that: she went into the world knowing that she could fly without fear, and if she failed, her clan would be there to rally round, pick her up, dust her off and help her get back on track. Interestingly, 25 years on, all her siblings are successful in their careers and their marriages.

Freedom to evolve

Fear can be overcome by rationalising it and adopting a different mindset. In some cases, though, fear can be deep-rooted and stem from trauma sometimes as far back as childhood. We are all made up of energy, and everything around us is made up of energy. In Chinese medicine the belief is that illness or fear is caused by energy being blocked. Emotional freedom technique (EFT) tapping was developed by a Stanford-trained engineer called Gary Craig. Craig was a student of Dr Roger Callahan, a psychologist and pioneer in cognitive and behaviour therapies. In EFT the tapping technique is called *chasing the energy*. When the meridians are tapped, the blockage is cleared and energy can flow freely.

I have witnessed the power of EFT tapping firsthand in a workshop. In the competitive landscape of professional growth, overcoming personal hurdles can often be the differentiator between stagnation and advancement. Take the case of Anna, a talented professional, whose fear of public speaking had become a formidable obstacle to her aspirations for promotion. Despite her expertise and dedication, the mere thought of addressing a crowd would trigger paralysing anxiety, limiting her ability to showcase her capabilities effectively.

At the workshop, Anna volunteered to go up on stage in front of the audience. The EFT therapist tapped on her pressure points and asked her to talk through what was coming up for her. It emerged that Anna's childhood experiences had left deep scars; her parents' admonishments to silence her voice, coupled with humiliating public reprimands, had instilled in her a profound fear of visibility. She had learned to retreat into solitude as a means of self-preservation. She avoided group settings and discussions to shield herself from further emotional harm. This ingrained response, though once having been a protective mechanism, now held her back from fully engaging in life's opportunities.

Remarkably, Anna's mind retained these memories – a testament to her innate capacity for self-preservation – even when the patterns the memories perpetuated were no longer beneficial. Through EFT tapping, Anna began to unravel her entrenched beliefs, reclaiming her voice and dismantling the barriers that had hindered her progress.

Facing our fears can often lead not only to greater opportunity but also to healing. Have you ever noticed, when you are worried about something you have put off addressing, that you get sick, have migraines or sleepless nights, or become clumsy?

Usually, when we have a fear of changing career or starting a business, we hold ourselves back, worrying we need to have perfected our skills first or gained years and years of experience before we make the leap. We see only success or failure and nothing in between. We convince ourselves we need to figure everything out from the get-go, putting pressure on ourselves to have the ultimate finished product and service before going to market. Perfectionism and analysis paralysis set in.

Businesses don't work this way. They are fluid, and they evolve and innovate. Here is a list of well-known successful brands, all of which started life selling something different before pivoting in response to a gap in the market or customer feedback:

- Marriott Hotels – started as a humble root-beer stand
- Wrigley's – started out packaging soap
- Samsung – originally exported noodles and dry fish
- American Express – harnessed the power of horses to deliver packages faster
- Netflix – rented out and sold physical DVD movies
- Amazon – started out as an online marketplace for books
- Tiffany – originally sold stationery
- Avon – sold books door to door
- YouTube – started life as a dating website

Another example of a limiting belief is when people think they are too old to change careers. Below are examples of well-known people who became success-ful later in life.

- Vera Wang, the New York fashion designer, is known across the globe, but she didn't launch her high-end label until she was 40.

- JK Rowling came up with the idea for her bestselling book series when she was 25 and working as a teacher, but it wasn't until she was 32 that *Harry Potter and the Philosopher's Stone* was published, and according to an article in *The Economic Times Magazine*, that only happened after it had been rejected 12 times by publishers.

- Cath Kidston was the owner of a second-hand furniture shop until the age of 45. As reported by the *Financial Times* in 2016, in 2010 Cath Kidston sold her design and retail company to investors for £25 million, while remaining on the board of directors.

- Samuel L Jackson – one of my favourite actors – was a social activist before becoming an actor in the 1970s, when he mostly held small roles in theatre and in movies. In his early forties, he landed his first major films, *School Daze* and *Do the Right Thing*, before being catapulted to stardom with *Pulp Fiction* in 1994. According to a 2011 *Business Insider* article, he's now made more money at the box office than any other actor alive.

- Ray Kroc was a businessperson and the force behind the global expansion of the McDonald's Corporation. As detailed in Britannica, in 1954 Kroc, a milkshake machine sales agent, learned that a small restaurant in San Bernardino,

California, run by Richard and Maurice McDonald, was using eight of his machines. In 1961, at the age of 59, Ray Kroc purchased the McDonald brothers' equity in the company and took control of the company.

EXERCISE: Reframing fear

Start this exercise by creating a list of your fears and doubts about changing your career:

- Consider all the worst-case scenarios and write them down on paper. Be specific.
- In a second column, write down the opportunity the change presents.
- In a third column, decide what action you would take to get back on track if the worst-case scenario did happen.
- In a fourth column, rate how likely the worst-case scenario is, on a scale of 1 (not likely) to 10 (highly likely).

Your list might look something like the example below.

This list will help you put each fear into perspective and realise that the worst-case outcome is unlikely or at least manageable.

Next, develop strategies to address each fear, reframe it and overcome it. It's important to jot down each fear and doubt so you can rationalise it. Seeing

it written down often makes it feel smaller and
more manageable.

Fear	Opportunity	Action	Likelihood
Failure of career change / new business	Learn new skills and try something new	Go back to a corporate job	4
Inability to pay my bills			
People's judgement			
Losing progression			
Giving up private medical, paid holidays, pension, sick pay			
Making a mistake			
Being visible			
Being too old to start over			
Lack of support			
Not being good enough			

Taking action

Often, when we are overwhelmed, overworked or underpaid, we are in a tornado of despair. We can't think clearly, and we've lost our sense of self. Through the long commutes, late nights, early starts and missed special occasions, our careers have become our identity. It can be tough enough to figure out what we want for dinner, never mind a career move.

Sometimes it's easiest to start with the questions:

- What don't you want?

- What is no longer serving you?

- What do you want less of?

- What energises you so that you want more?

Reflecting on these questions is a good starting point. It can take a bit of practice to go deeper to find the answers. Doing so may stir emotions and fears – some of which you have conveniently locked away in a box with a nice, neat bow on it – because opening Pandora's box may mean having to face up to difficult conversations and decisions. Now is the time to stop procrastinating, stop talking about it, stop daydreaming and take action, because what is the alternative? The biggest risk is that 12 months from now you will still be in the same place – stuck.

EXERCISE: Regrets list vs gains list

List the regrets you have or would have if you didn't change careers.

Alongside this, make another list of all the things you will gain by taking a leap.

Here are some examples from my list, which might help trigger ideas for you:

- Having more time with my family, pets and friends
- Doing work I enjoy
- Exploring other paid opportunities, eg speaking gigs, programmes
- Having time to write my book
- Meeting new people and collaborating, eg networking events, Chamber of Commerce, coworking
- Having more time for self-care, going to the gym, walks on the beach
- Flexibility so I can work abroad
- Learning new skills, eg podcasting, online courses
- Revisiting passions and hobbies and exploring new interests, eg art, reading, horse riding, yoga, swimming

Summary

When considering a change of career, it helps to recognise that the most likely obstacle will be your own limiting beliefs. This chapter has given you new tools to overcome your fears, including naming and disregarding your frog. Completing the exercises on addressing your fears will bring you closer to taking action.

The Maverick Letters

Kieran McMahon, KMF and the Be a Better Man online fitness programme

Dear Founder,

I am going to start my story at a big turning point in my life, five days before my 21st birthday in 2008, when my mam passed away. I was the eldest of five, and despite having future plans to move abroad after university, I felt a sense of obligation to stay at home to help my dad with my four younger siblings. However, in one of my last conversations with my mam, she asked me to promise that I would leave Ireland and follow what I wanted to do. I am from a tiny, remote rural townland in the west of Ireland, called Querrin. By townland, I mean I am from the countryside – there is no town and no shops. In other words, I am from 'the sticks'.

My 21st birthday gift from my mam, which I received a few days after she passed, was a leather suitcase with the motto 'Pursue, Persist, Persevere' engraved on it. This is my company's motto today.

Despite feeling guilty, I had a promise to keep, and off I went to work as a schoolteacher in Abu Dhabi. From 2008 to 2019, I worked as a teacher and climbed up the leadership ladder to become a head of department in a private school. Life in Abu Dhabi was good. I was living in a country which had glorious weather 365 days of the year. I had a beautiful apartment on the 55th floor of a skyscraper, which was paid for by my school. I had zero tax to pay, and I was making good money. To top it off, I had 12 weeks of holidays every year. Pretty sweet, right?

But…

There was always a but. I wasn't fulfilled, and I had no control over how I worked. I remember being stuck in traffic one evening in 2016, after a long evening of doing private tutoring (for extra cash to pay for my next exotic holiday) and thinking to myself, How long do I want to do this for?

In short, I felt burnt out and unfulfilled. My job was 'fine', but that was all it was. I lived for the weekends and my holidays. The years were whizzing by, I was almost 30, and I knew deep down I wanted to make a change.

Now, I am an educator at heart. I enjoy teaching and helping people, and I love to learn about topics that interest me. I have always been into fitness and, from a young age, have had a strong desire to look and feel good. It was on that car journey home that something clicked. I decided there and then that I would align my highest values of fitness and education together and do what I wanted to do. Instead of teaching English to 18-year-olds, I decided to teach fitness and nutrition to adults. I also wanted to create something that allowed me to incorporate my other value of 'freedom', and that is exactly what I set out to do.

I became a qualified personal trainer and started running free bootcamp and one-to-one personal training classes for teachers, alongside my job, over that first year. This gave me loads of experience, increased confidence and a tonne of results. In my second year, I started charging for my services and got my personal training business to a point where I was getting paid enough to live without needing to touch my teaching salary.

On the second day of the new school term in 2018, I handed in my resignation letter nine months ahead of time. I needed the accountability and was now all in. That final year in full-time employment was a tough one. I gave up alcohol, didn't go out, and put all of my time and money into coaching clients and investing in business mentors. I had zero business experience and needed to learn from people who had been there and done it.

I decided to move back to Ireland in 2019, and I transitioned my business online. I had 15 clients paying me enough so

I didn't have to look for a new job. I had achieved what I had set out to do over an 18-month period.

Today I have a team of six, and my company coaches men in 20 countries around the world. Our mission is to educate and coach men into the best physical and mental shape of their lives while still prioritising their fun, family and finances. From being in the education world for over ten years and going through all the levels of education myself, I knew there was a gap in understanding life skills. I didn't have a clue of how to manage my money or take care of my mental health when I finished university, and so many men I speak to are the same. I now see it as my mission or purpose to teach men how to thrive in these areas.

You might read this and think, 'That all makes sense, but I don't know what my purpose is as I am not really passionate about anything in particular. What do I do?'

My advice on this is simple. People don't start passion projects or know what their purpose is when they start. People start businesses doing things they enjoy doing or are good at, and the passion part comes when they start growing. Growing the business and creating the impact becomes the passion, and it only comes after you start. Starting is the hardest part. For me, I had an interest in education and fitness and found a job that combined both. Everything else grew from there.

Today I am free, grateful for the life I live. I spend most of the year in the south of England but also have the freedom to travel around the globe multiple times a year to places like Dubai or the US to hold client events, or to more exotic places like Bali to take time out. I can visit my family in Ireland whenever I want or take a trip with my girlfriend in Pedro, our camper van. I now live life on my terms doing what I want, when I want. I combine work with play and don't see one as separate from the other.

To get me to this point, a number of things have hugely helped:

- ***Invest in mentors and coaches.*** *Find someone who is living the life you want, pay for their time, and learn the pathway and skills that got them to where they are. I have spent tens of thousands of pounds on my personal development since starting and it has been the single biggest reason for my success.*

- ***Take care of your health.*** *I now work with male entrepreneurs and business owners whose energy and health are through the floor because they are burnt out. Building a business is incredibly exciting and rewarding but also highly stressful at times. You need to take regular breaks to be at your best. Never sacrifice your health for anything.*

- ***Surround yourself with like-minded people who are doing what you do.*** *Running a business can be lonely, and people who don't run a business don't* *really get you. There are loads of free community groups online you can join, or invest in a personal development programme that has a community element to it.*

- **Be clear on what you are willing to sacrifice, and communicate that with the people that matter the most such as a partner, friends or family.** *To create a business on your terms, you have to be willing to sacrifice certain things, despite what business gurus will tell you on social media. Whether that is your free time, savings, alcohol, etc, you have to be willing to part ways with certain things, especially at the start. As mentioned earlier, I gave up alcohol for a full year, and it was one of the best things I did.*

- **Not everyone will support you on your new venture in the beginning.** *See this as a sign of success. I used to get a lot of people making fun of me for my social media posts or for not going out drinking. Understand that if you want a new life, you will need new standards. View any negative comments towards your new life as a sign of success. Most people don't like change, so if you are not receiving any kickbacks, you are probably not changing enough!*

I hope this has inspired you to take that leap of faith you know is deep down inside of you. The only thing that stops people from taking real action is themselves and their beliefs.

Remember, if a guy from a townland in the west of Ireland with no business background can do it, so can you.

To your future success.

Pursue, persist, persevere.

Kieran
www.kmfitnesscoaching.com

PART TWO
GETTING UNSTUCK

THREE

Identify Your Vision And Values

Understanding your vision and values is fundamental when you are considering a career change. Your vision acts as a guiding light, illuminating the path forward and infusing your journey with purpose and direction. It defines the future you aspire to create, whether that involves aligning your career with your passions, or making a meaningful impact in your chosen field. Similarly, your values serve as a moral compass, guiding you towards decisions and pursuits that resonate with your authentic self. When your career aligns with your values, you experience a profound sense of fulfilment and purpose, transcending mere professional success to lead a life rich in meaning and significance.

Moreover, clarity on your vision and values empowers you to navigate career transitions with confidence and conviction. By honing in on what truly matters to you, you cultivate a sense of purpose that outweighs external pressures and societal expectations.

In this chapter I'll introduce more exercises to help you figure out what is important to you and arrive at an idea of what you would like to achieve and the legacy you want to leave behind.

It's time for exploring and experimenting. Let's dive in.

EXERCISE: Start with the Why

This exercise will help you determine what really motivates you most. Start with the following question:

Why do you want a career change?

You might reply, for example, *Because I hate my job.*

Why do you hate your job?

Because I don't want to be doing this until I retire.

Why?

Keep asking why as many times as you can, until you've hit on a root cause or have an 'aha' moment.

Your answers might suggest what you don't want in your career anymore and how it's making you feel.

Mindfully check in throughout the day and ask yourself the following questions:

- Am I enjoying what I'm doing right now?
- What is it that I'm enjoying doing specifically?
- What else?
- What do I really enjoy and love in my job, career and life?
- What personal and professional tasks or activities do I really enjoy or feel a buzz when I am doing them?
- What do I get so engrossed in that I put off other things? Is it something about what I'm doing? Something else? What else?
- What produces the highest ratio of satisfaction and abundance versus the amount of time spent on it?

Complete the sentence: *I am at my best when I am [doing]* ...

Keep asking yourself, *WHAT? What else? What more?*

EXERCISE: Future Self

Close your eyes and imagine you are 80 years old and at your birthday party.

- Who do you see?
- What does your home look like?
- What have you achieved?
- What are people saying about you?
- What are you most proud of?
- What do you regret doing and wish you had done?

As you reflect on these questions, notice what feelings are coming up for you.

The next step is to get clear on your vision. Understanding what isn't serving you or bringing you joy can help to determine what you do want. For example, in your imagined future, perhaps you work remotely and, now that you are not commuting, you can dedicate time to walking or jogging in the morning. You can be home in the early evenings to sit down and enjoy a meal with your family and spend more time with your pets.

Perhaps you are also missing the connection of colleagues and feeling isolated. In that case, you need to explore coworking, join a networking group or work from a local coffee shop for a few hours.

Think too about someone you admire, who has the lifestyle you want. It might be someone famous – an influencer, founder, neighbour, colleague, relative or friend. Jot down what it is about their life you want.

Once you gain a clear understanding of your vision, it becomes your guiding compass – your North Star. It empowers you to establish precise and significant goals and take purposeful actions to achieve your ambitions.

Seeing is believing

Looking at images primes our brains to grasp opportunities we may not otherwise have noticed. This process is called *value tagging*. It imprints important things onto our unconscious and filters out unnecessary information. In other words, we place higher value on images than written or spoken words, and the more we observe those images, the more important they become.

Our brain sees little difference between something happening and a strongly imagined vision of it. Therefore, visualise things as already happening. When I decided to write this book, I envisioned what it would look like – the book cover, the pages, the weight of it, what the message would be and how the book would help people. I imagined it on bookshelves. I imagined how it would feel to be a published author.

Normally, when you think of doing something new, it might feel scary or fearful. This can bring on a stress response, releasing cortisol in your body. However, if you repeatedly look at images of your goals, your brain will no longer see them as new, which will allow you to take healthy risks and embrace new opportunities.

Creating a vision board is a positive mood booster. A vision board is also known as a dream board, action board, mood board or journey board. It visually represents your desired career and lifestyle and serves as a tangible reminder of your goals. The act of writing and creating by hand is generally a much more powerful creation process than typing, copying and pasting, so step away from the laptop and create your vision board with card, pens and magazine clippings. By going through the creative process, you will be reflecting, visualising, meditating and journalling, which energises your brain. The vision-board process of creating is part of the journey, setting your intentions from the start.

EXERCISE: Vision board

This is a fun, future-focused exercise. Set aside time to work on your vision board, and don't rush to complete it all in one go – you can add to it over time.

You will need an A3 piece of card or paper, magazines, coloured pens, scissors and glue.

Go with your heart – it's entirely up to you what you want to add to your vision board. You might want to include:

- Travel destinations that are on your bucket list
- Hobbies and interests
- Things to do with health, love or money
- Affirmations and motivational quotes that ring true with you

Place your vision board somewhere you will see it every day. That might be above your desk or your bed, or on the hallway wall. You might even hang it as a piece of art on your living room wall.

Values are vital

In our journey of self-discovery and career exploration, our values are one of the most potent guiding forces. You may not always realise it, but your values are your guiding principles. They act as your compass, directing you along fulfilling and meaningful paths.

Often, when my coaching clients come to me, they cannot figure out why they are feeling stuck. They are bright, intelligent, accomplished and rational women and men. They have followed society's formula: getting a good education and climbing the corporate ladder. Most of them have married, bought a house in the suburbs, have kids and are well travelled... and then they hit a wall. Suddenly there is a void.

Initially, they think the problem lies with the company they work for, and that they will find a new challenge and lease of life if they just change employers. They therefore go about dusting off their CV, applying for jobs and interviewing. They get an offer, perhaps more money and prestige, and they convince themselves they have found the solution. Six months later, though, they realise the void is still there. They persuade themselves they need a bigger house, more holidays, perhaps a new haircut, possibly a new partner. Alas, the void still hasn't gone, and they are at a loss. On paper they are considered successful, but in reality, their carefully curated life has left them feeling unfulfilled.

I like to think of that void as a gift. That sense of feeling unfulfilled – that inner voice telling you to act – is simply your unconscious knocking on your door. In most cases it's because there is a misalignment, and you are not being true to your values.

Values are within us from an early age. At school I was always getting into hot water for sticking up for the underdog. My mother looked perplexed as she came back from one parents' evening. My form tutor discussed my grades with her then told her, 'Ms Willocks, your daughter will either end up in prison or running the country.' Fortunately for everyone, including me, neither of those scenarios has come true. Unsurprisingly, though, justice is one of my core values.

In addition to our core values, we also have our career values, which can change over time. For example, when I started out in my career, work–life balance wasn't that important to me. I was young, ambitious and full of energy. I was working in the hospitality industry, where long, unsociable hours were part of the territory. I worked hard and played hard, with very little sleep in between. As I became older, my outlook changed, mainly due to me burning out. I therefore made a conscious choice to move into contract catering, which gave me a more structured working pattern, including weekends off.

FOLLOWING VALUES

Work–life balance became increasingly important for Joanna and Victor Gould, both 34, from London. They wanted to spend more time in nature and with family, so they quit the rat race and left their corporate jobs in favour of living life on their own terms, travelling the UK while running a café from their narrowboat.

Steph and Mat Trott – 30 and 34, respectively – from Sussex, decided to retire 30 years early. In 2018 they quit their jobs to move to Greece and create a homestead, to live a more eco-conscious and sustainable life.

Emily Campbell and her husband, Dan Regan, escaped burnout to be closer to nature and become caretakers of Great Blasket Island, a 1,100-acre island off the west coast of Ireland. Their advice is to have no regrets and take action.

Our values alter over time, sometimes due to life-changing events. One of my clients, Kelly, was struggling to switch companies. She was applying for roles that looked great on paper and being invited to interviews, but her heart wasn't in the process. We spent a session unpacking her values. Kelly had become vegan several years earlier after volunteering for an animal welfare charity. Veganism had become a core value, and her career values had shifted. She now wanted to work in an environment where veganism was at the heart of her employer's mission statement and values.

> This realisation was a lightbulb moment for Kelly.
> She now understood why she had been feeling so
> unfulfilled at work: it lacked meaning. That void was
> also the reason she was applying for job roles but not
> accepting them.

Core values are the things that make you who you are – the principles by which you want to live your life, professionally and personally. Recognising your values allows you to make better choices, meaning you can prioritise things that give you greater satisfaction and fulfilment.

In an interview with podcaster Steven Bartlett, the entrepreneur and vice chair of West Ham, Baroness Karren Brady, said that she knew at the age of 18 that ambition, determination and integrity were important to her, and that, at 52, they are still her core values.

The right culture for you

In collectivist cultures, community values prevail, which emphasises harmony and cooperation. Individualistic cultures, meanwhile, prioritise personal freedom and achievement. Understanding these cultural variations is crucial to fostering intercultural communication and inclusivity, especially in the workplace. If, like me, you don't like unpredictable change and navigating ambiguity, working in a startup may send you into a frenzy. Conversely, if you thrive in an ever-changing environment with little structure, then working in a large, corporate environment is not going to be your jam. An SME (small to medium-sized enterprise) will be a better compromise.

Historical, economic and political contexts can also shape societal values over time. A perfect example is how lockdown has impacted flexible working and the rise of remote working. According to a 2022 report by consulting firm McKinsey, almost half of job seekers are now ready to re-prioritise their career, with 32% admitting the pandemic has made them reassess what they're looking for. This has led to the term 'great resignation'.

Ask yourself:

- When I was living my best life, what was I doing?

- What was it about that time that makes it so significant?

- During which moments was I at my lowest point?

- What was happening?

- Which environments do I thrive in?

If you are unsure of your values, the following exercise will help you to determine what you most need to focus on.

EXERCISE: Like, love, loathe

On a piece of paper, start by making three columns –
Like, Love and Loathe – to document your feelings
about your current job.

Think about the environment, culture, pace, people,
work–life balance and training, and the work itself. In
addition to all the positive points, which you add to
the Like and Loathe columns, list any adverse aspects
under 'Loathe'. Perhaps you work long hours and crave
more work–life balance. Maybe you are in a sales-
driven environment that focuses on metrics, but you
are more motivated by relationship building. You may
be in a financially unstable startup environment, while
you crave career stability and financial security. It
might be that you loathe the commute, job insecurity,
lack of progression and micromanaging in your
current position.

Next, consider how each of these negative factors
is impacting you. The long hours might mean time
away from your family and pets, and less time for
self-care. The commute is probably costly and eating
into your spare time. Perhaps you are not recognised
and valued for your contribution, which can be
demoralising. If your work culture is toxic, it is no
doubt having a damaging impact on your morale.
Perhaps you are having to pick up extra work for the
same pay while working in a stressful environment and
feeling undervalued.

This list will be personal to you. After you have written
down everything you think of, comparing the number of
likes and loves with the things you loathe will give you

a clear picture of your satisfaction in your current job. Usually, when you loathe something, it's because it is misaligned with your values.

The following exercise will help you to examine your values more closely and to determine the types of companies and careers that will bring you the most fulfilment.

EXERCISE: Past, present and future

Take time to think through all the points listed below, again noting down everything you think of.

Begin by reflecting on your past experiences, both personal and professional:

- What have you enjoyed the most in your previous roles or activities?
- What made you feel fulfilled and motivated?

Consider your strengths, skills, and values:

- What skills do you excel at?
- What values are essential to you in a career?

Imagine yourself in the future, say 12 months to 10 years from now:

- What does your ideal career look like?
- Where are you working, what are you doing and who are you working with?

Envision your day-to-day life, including work responsibilities, work–life balance, and any other factors important to you:

- Which values are being met?
- Which values are missing from your current career?
- Which of your career choices have met your values or closely align with your values?

Now list potential careers that would meet your values. You are going to explore these further.

Once you've identified the values you prioritise, it's essential to assess whether they align with potential employers and their stated values. Examine job descriptions for insights into any company's culture, and explore employers' websites for information on their values.

If a company's values are elusive or difficult to discern, this may signal potential shortcomings in their practices. Conversely, while many companies proudly showcase their core values, it's crucial to go beyond the surface and verify that these values are genuinely reflected in the company's day-to-day operations. Employee and candidate reviews on Glassdoor can give a good insight into the organisation.

Summary

Identifying your vision and values is an essential step when you are designing your ideal future. Understanding what motivates you most in life and imagining your idea future will illuminate what you need to work towards. A vision board will help you to decide what's most important to you as well as what you need to avoid.

It's only when you are true to your own personal values and vision that you can seek your ideal new environment and fully flourish.

The Maverick Letters

Anja Poehlmann, photographer, filmmaker, storyteller

Dear creator,

I'd love to tell you that I had a precise plan for my future since I was a teenager and that I created a clear path that led me to where I am today.

No, I was never one of those kids in school who knew what they wanted from life. Instead, a reality TV show on MTV inspired me to move to the other side of the world at the age of 23. In a moment of courage, I took an opportunity to move to Hawaii for an unpaid internship at a TV station. Because I am from East Germany, Hawaii was as far from my imagination as the moon in terms of 'a place to visit someday'.

I spent half a year working in a creative job in a foreign country, meeting wonderful people I'm still friends with almost 20 years later, making my own choices and having to take responsibility for my life. It was the best experience of my life.

The six months went fast. I moved back to Germany, found a job in video production and started a side hustle in photography. Work was busy and exciting, but my life felt like something was missing.

I eventually decided to pack up and leave Germany again – this time for the UK – with some savings in the bank and no plan for what would come next.

In 2015 I started my dream job: telling the stories of international students in the UK through videos. I travelled up and down the country; met 19-year-olds who knew who they wanted to be; and got a chance to get a whole new perspective on education, determination and the challenges of life. However, after a few years, I started feeling restricted by company politics and processes that weren't always in line with my own preferences. This time, my life felt great, but my work felt like something was missing.

I didn't feel like I could experiment enough. The restrictions of working within someone else's framework – representing someone else's values and chasing someone else's plans – became overwhelmingly frustrating.

I didn't grow up with a role model or anyone in my wider or closer circle running their own business, which means I never accepted it as a viable option, until my friends – freelance wedding photographers I met through my photography side hustle – encouraged me to consider it.

I am now a photographer and filmmaker for families and small businesses. My values are connection, honesty and freedom. I can see them in my work and the clients I get to work with.

Working in a corporate job felt safe and secure: regular pay checks, regulated working hours, clear responsibilities, benefits.

Running your own business is the exact opposite: it's scary and comes with challenges I never saw coming.

You know what else happens when you go your own way? You make your own rules. You work hours that suit your own rhythm. You learn things you never thought you'd understand. You grow faster than you could imagine.

My business gave me the opportunity to really understand how I like to work, what my own values are and how I can live them through my work. Running a business is not easy, and over the past years, I had moments of doubt (thanks, COVID). Four years later, though, I'm still here, paying my bills with the money my business makes.

I learned that I get frustrated when something doesn't align with my values. It triggers me, and instead of trying to push through, I now have the chance to re-evaluate and analyse those triggers – and then change what doesn't fit.

My advice to you is: find out what your own values are and how you can implement them in your work life. Working for yourself might be the hardest job you'll ever have, but it will be on your terms. You've got to take responsibility for your own decisions to live a life where the thought of work doesn't fill you with dread but with joy.

Good luck on your own journey.

Anja
www.anjapoehlmann.com

Chris Bone, Adventure Solos

I'm in my early forties, and I used to work in investment and finance. I now run a company called Adventure Solos.

'A good job' is typically code for, 'pays well'. It doesn't mention happiness or life satisfaction. By those standards, I used to have a good job. I had a six-figure income. Now I earn far less, but I believe it's a better job, if we were to use the definition correctly. It makes me happy; I believe I'm helping people, and that is fulfilling. It's also mine – I'm working for myself, in control of my own destiny, and I'm proud of what I've built so far. I wasn't particularly unhappy in my previous career.

I had enjoyed it for a long time, but it got to the point where I no longer found it fulfilling. I wanted to do my own thing instead. I had no idea what I would do. I ended up creating what became Adventure Solos by simply doing what I loved – what I believed in – and letting things evolve.

When I left the corporate world, I'd recently bought a house and had some money saved to refurbish it. I spent nine months doing that, then I needed to start earning money again. I had always been into the outdoors and would plan trips for myself and a few friends for holidays. In a way, I was turning my passion into my profession.

Things evolved. At first the 'solos' part was the tagline rather than the name of the company (this meant people could book on by themselves for group adventures – you don't need to convince your other half, friends or family to come too). Over time, you realise it's important to pick your niches, so this went into the name. Similarly, the events are designed for people in their thirties, forties and fifties, which tends to mean people have things in common and sometimes similar life experiences. It's important to figure out your own niches, then you know who your market is rather than it just being 'anyone and everyone'.

Early on, one of the guests on an event asked me what my values were. I had no idea what she meant or how to answer. It is something I've thought about a lot, though, and I think what this really means is, What's important to you in your life? For me, that's easier to answer. These values are then definitely reflected in the events offered through Adventure Solos. A few key ones are:

- *Being around people, having community, building relationships and having a sense of belonging*

- *Living less materialistic lives, focused on experiences and being happy*

- *Being outdoors, spending time in nature, having adventures, staying active and challenging oneself*

I think these things clearly feed through from my personal life to my work life. Some of this might happen naturally if you're creating your own business, but it's useful to be aware of them to help you identify and orientate sound values you are passionate about, and to ensure your offerings are genuine reflections of you. It's important to inject a bit of personality into your new life and business; people can relate to that.

For me, there were practical things that made taking the leap easier. I had been earning good money, I lived a relatively modest lifestyle (the things that are important to me don't cost a lot), and I didn't have dependants. I was happy to take the risk, although with lockdown coming along after a few months, there were some tough years early on. You'll know in your heart what you want to do – you just need to find a way to make it happen. A few pieces of advice:

- *Do something that helps people, including offering some stuff for free, to help get them started and engaged.*

- *Test your new life/business/idea while you're still in your old life. See what works or doesn't and go from there.*

- *Marketing is key for a B2C company. You can have the best offering in the world, but if people don't know you exist, no one is going to stumble across your website/product/service. Have an idea of how people may find you / how you can find them.*

- *Try to step back regularly and ask yourself not what will get you an extra sale, but what would double your sales.*

- *Finally, stay focused. It's easy to have a million ideas and be trying to be Chief Everything Officer when you're starting out. Almost anything you do will add value or improve things. You run the risk of having no strategy or work–life balance if you take this approach, though. Instead, find a way of ranking or prioritising your ideas, making sure they are on strategy, deliverable and if/how you will know if they are working for you or not.*

Best of luck, and feel free to reach out if you think I can help you.

Chris
www.adventuresolos.com

FOUR

Find Your Fire Power

The dynamics of our job requirements are evolving faster than ever before, and the future of work is shifting towards prioritising transferable skills over specific job roles or industries. These skills transcend job titles and fields, allowing us to carry them from one role to another. A 2022 analysis report on LinkedIn revealed a 25% change in the essential skills for an average job since 2015. The 2024 LinkedIn report *The Future of Recruiting* states that 75% of hiring professionals agree that skills-first hiring will play an increasingly pivotal role in the future of recruitment than higher education qualifications.

Consequently, mastering the art of showcasing your transferable skills is becoming essential for shaping your career path. By thoroughly identifying and cataloguing your transferable skills, you may discover new opportunities you had not previously considered.

According to research conducted by Statista in 2023, 93% of employers consider soft skills crucial in their hiring decisions, highlighting the desire for candidates who can contribute a versatile set of skills to their organisations. Soft skills include character traits and interpersonal talents, including:

- Emotional intelligence
- Critical thinking
- Analytic thinking and problem solving
- Effective communication
- Adaptability and flexibility
- Collaboration and teamwork
- Time management
- Attention to detail and quality assurance
- Leadership and management

Hard skills tend to be more quantifiable abilities, including functional or technical skills such as:

- Foreign languages
- Graphic design
- Sales management

- Project management

- Computer skills such as data analysis, coding, search engine optimisation

Soft and hard skills extend beyond your most recent role and hold significance at any career stage. Transferable skills may stem, for example, from previous leadership roles, volunteer work, side hustles, language proficiency, sports participation, interpersonal aptitude and hobbies. The benefits of these skills include:

- Facilitating personal growth within your current role

- Enabling your involvement in projects and opportunities of interest

- Serving as valuable assets when marketing yourself for a new job or industry

Your skills will evolve and adapt over time. Whether you are an employee or self-employed, your skills will become your currency for remaining relevant in an ever-changing market.

Identifying crucial skills

It is important to understand how the global market is evolving and how it will influence changes to the industry you are working in or intending to move into. Look at job descriptions in the specific field you are considering. Review the skills and experience that clients and employers are targeting, and determine any skills gaps you might need to address.

While skills are not static and will evolve and adapt, they are not always going to be suited to each environment or every stage of a company's life cycle. For example, it is typical for founders to remain as CEOs once their company reaches a certain point in its growth trajectory. According to a study in 2021 by Hendricks et al, published in *Harvard Business Review*, the lifespan of a founder CEO in a high-trajectory growth company is benchmarked at around six years. After this period, they often find greater success in other roles or by exiting the business altogether.

The qualities that make a great entrepreneur – a willingness to experiment, a penchant for risk-taking and visionary thinking, and a strategic mindset – do not necessarily align with the skill set required for an effective CEO. The resourcefulness and can-do spirit that fuelled the initial stages of the business may not seamlessly transition to running a multimillion-dollar enterprise with a sizeable workforce. Frequently, though, founders may not recognise the full extent of their transferable skills. As your company expands, the skills needed for leadership must evolve in tandem.

Selling our strengths short

As humans, we tend to focus more on our shortcomings than our strengths. It's unsurprising when you think about most people's experiences at school. Most of us are taught from an early age that we should excel in all subjects, to be an all-rounder. Unfortunately, when we excel only in one certain area, that is often met with indifference from parents and educators rather than that skill being nurtured and developed with further time and investment. Successful entrepreneurs, however, will tell us to focus on one thing and master it.

Imagine what greatness could be achieved if your potential was recognised, nurtured and celebrated; if you only had to focus on the subjects you thrived in. You would acquire deeper knowledge, honing your skills and passion, and that might set you on a different and more exciting career path.

According to the report *Employees Who Use Their Strengths Outperform Those Who Don't*, by advisory firm Gallup, if we are not in our 'strengths zone', we are six times less engaged. Reflecting on times when I haven't been able to use my skills:

- I felt demotivated, demoralised and disengaged.

- I didn't feel valued by my employer.

- I was less creative, and my input and contributions would diminish.

'What are your strengths?' is a common interview question, and yet it's something I have found most candidates struggle to answer. Most of us are not used to describing our own or others' strengths. We are more likely to say, 'Mallika is passionate about marketing,' than, 'Mallika's strength is running marketing campaigns.'

How motivating would it be if, in the workplace, you were known for your strengths? Imagine you were in a meeting about a new client project, and without hesitating, your boss looked at you and said, 'Your strength is numbers. This is an important account, which would be benefit from your expertise.' Wouldn't that feel great?

Unfortunately, far too many of us spend a lifetime headed in the wrong direction, without uncovering our natural talents and potential. This is why it is vital you discover and develop your strengths as early as possible. Understanding your strengths will help you identify career paths that allow you to leverage yourself in areas where you naturally excel.

Think of skills as abilities and talents that you do well, have learned to hone over time, and have an expertise in. Your strengths are characteristics that enable you to perform at your best and give you an energy buzz. They are your unique selling point – your superpowers – which, combined with your values, make up what I call your Fire Power.

EXERCISE: Your superpowers

Divide an A4 piece of paper into two columns, headed 'Hard skills' (eg technical skills) and 'Soft skills' (eg communication, leadership). List the skills you possess in both columns.

Now think of a time when you felt really energised and on form, when you were at your best and thriving, personally or professionally:

- Where were you?
- Who were you with?
- What were you doing?
- What *specifically* were you doing?
- What did you enjoy about it?
- How did you feel when doing it?
- What were you thinking at the time?
- What else is useful to note?

Now reflect on past achievements, projects or tasks where you excelled. Identify what skills or qualities enabled your success and add them to your sheet.

Think about any positive feedback or compliments you've received from your colleagues, boss, customers or clients regarding your work performance. Identify what skills and qualities these might represent and add them to your sheet.

Look for recurring patterns or commonalities among the skills and qualities identified in the previous steps. These are likely your strengths. You may wish to refer to these later when exploring which careers you may consider moving into.

My old school friend, David, whom I have known for 30 years, told me once that I was the most determined person he knew. At the time, I had recently been in a training programme for coaches. When we were discussing communication, someone remarked that I had a nice communication style – they thought it was structured and well spoken. I was stunned and flattered – this wasn't something I had previously considered as one of my strengths.

Constructive feedback can offer valuable insights and help you assess whether your current career path aligns with your purpose and goals. Reach out to friends, mentors, colleagues and peers, asking them what they perceive as your strengths in a professional context. If possible, have a discussion with your boss to gain insights from their perspective. You might be surprised by people's responses.

You may also consider taking psychometric assessment for personality and strengths. For example, DISC, Myers-Briggs and StrengthsFinder can be useful online tools to gain insights into careers that might suit certain behavioural styles and strengths.

Compare the different sources of information, and consolidate your strengths into a final, refined list. Start applying your identified strengths in your workplace, and observe how they positively impact your performance and outcomes. Be open to refining and adjusting your list of strengths, based on real-world application and feedback. Understanding your strengths is an ongoing process, and it's important to continuously reflect on and refine your understanding.

Seeking your inner genius

Let's take it one step further, because knowing your strengths is important, but it does not necessarily mean you have discovered your sweet spot. One challenge you likely face isn't a lack of expertise but rather that you are proficient in lots of different areas. While it's positive to be skilled at many things, it still presents a dilemma. If you are someone who has a thirst for knowledge in new areas and is constantly taking courses in different topics, your extensive knowledge can become a source of paralysis as choosing between good, better and best becomes challenging. The solution lies in discovering your genius zone – the space where you can offer something genuinely unique.

In his book *The Big Leap*, Gay Hendricks encourages us to evaluate our lives in four distinct categories:

1. Incompetence

2. Competence

3. Excellence

4. Genius

Hendricks proposes that we experience greater fulfilment and happiness when we dedicate more time to activities within our genius zone. Tasks in which you are competent or even excellent are probably where your competitors are less capable. The key to creating unique value lies in focusing on activities within your genius zone. Hallmarks of this zone include:

- It involves activities that only you can perform, or in which you've invested 10,000 hours of deliberate practice to achieve exceptional proficiency.

- It includes those activities where you are more likely to be within a flow state – a state where you're fully absorbed in your work, oblivious to time as you tap into the abilities that come naturally to you.

- It is distinctively tailored to your individuality and personality traits. The genius zone involves merging your areas of utmost confidence with your calling or life's purpose, which might even include activities you hadn't previously thought you would enjoy.

The essence of your genius zone lies in harnessing your innate talents and directing them towards your passion, ensuring that your work becomes genuinely enjoyable for you.

In practical terms, what does this mean? You might be really good at marketing, while your hobby is surfing, which you are passionate about. Combining the two may well be your genius zone. Surfing is something you enjoy, which doesn't feel like work; and combining that with marketing is rare, making you more competitive.

Other benefits of identifying your genius zone include:

- It significantly enhances your ability to concentrate and generate content ideas.

- It simplifies the process of identifying your target audience and enables easier and more effective communication with them.

- It adds depth and value to your service for your audience, making your contribution fully meaningful and fulfilling.

Perhaps you're good at your job, but you just don't love it anymore. During my time as both a recruiter and a coach, I have come across people that have excelled in their careers, climbed the corporate ladder and become accomplished at what they do. They are operating in their *excellence zone*. They may be motivated to continue down this route because it's comfortable, they can do the job with their eyes closed and it pays the bills. However, they're not operating in their *genius zone* because, deep down, their work doesn't bring them joy, and the cracks start to set in.

If this happens to you, you won't be showing up as your authentic self. It's likely you will start turning up late to work, not participating in work events and becoming withdrawn in meetings. After a while, these changes will be noticed by your colleagues and boss, bonuses might start to become smaller, and that promotion will no longer be on the table. Perhaps not getting the promotion is a relief, though, because it means not having to dedicate more time to the job that no longer thrills you.

When coaching clients come to me, their main problem isn't that they are unaware that they feel unfulfilled; it's that they don't know what their genius zone is or how to go about finding it. These are smart people who fix problems every day, but they can't seem to get out of the mud when it comes to career happiness. This is normal. After all, a career is about more than just progression, development, colleagues and status. It's how we feed ourselves; put a roof over our heads; and pay for our kids' school trips and education, vet bills and health care emergencies. It's how we survive.

Finding your genius zone

Below is a simple exercise to help you identify your genius zone and to adapt your life to take full advantage of it.

EXERCISE: Getting in the flow

Think of some recent times where you felt like you were in flow – so completely absorbed and focused that you lost track of everything around you.

Write down what you were thinking of during these times in as much detail as you can, pinpointing how you felt and why.

Monitor your performance to develop the habit of nurturing your genius. Keep track of any time you spend in this zone, your level of happiness and your confidence.

Seek ways to integrate your genius zone into your workflow. To redirect more energy towards your genius zone, re-evaluate your priorities. Delegate or outsource other tasks to team members or freelancers excelling in those areas.

Working in your genius zone will likely create a ripple effect, fostering positive changes throughout your business. With your enjoyment of work, you gain more time for strategic thinking, enhancing overall team efficiency. Encourage your team to find their genius zones, creating a workplace that is not only fun and rewarding for you but for everyone. Integrate your genius zone into the business structure to elevate its overall wellbeing. Work should be an extension of yourself, not just a means to pay bills or a daily dread. Consistently performing at this level will inspire and uplift your team, further encouraging them to find their own genius zones.

> ## YOGA GENIUS
>
> Mays Al-Ali found her genius zone when she transitioned from a successful job in advertising to pursue a career in yoga and naturopathic medicine. She was spurred on to do so after experiencing burnout twice. During this period, she suffered with fatigue, hair loss, digestive issues and skin problems. Eventually, she relocated to Ibiza to host yoga retreats. Although this has meant letting go of job insecurity, Mays is happier, healthier and finds her new career so much more rewarding.

EXERCISE: SWOT analysis

First, consider these questions:

- **Strengths:** What are your Fire Power skills, experience, attributes and best characteristics?
- **Weaknesses:** What do you consider to be your weaknesses, or areas you have not yet developed?
- **Opportunities:** What resources do you have access to?
- **Threats:** What might stop you from working in your genius zone?

Draw a SWOT analysis quadrant for yourself, similar to the one below.

Work through the questions listed in each square.

STRENGTHS	WEAKNESSES
What is your Fire Power?	What is holding you back?
What do others see as your strengths?	What do others see as your weakness?
What unique personal resources can you leverage?	What do you resist or avoid doing because of a lack of confidence?

OPPORTUNITIES	THREATS
What opportunities are open to you?	What commitments might get in the way?
How can you turn your Fire Power into opportunities?	Could any of your weaknesses lead to threats?
What resources are available to you?	What is your competition doing?

Summary

Now that you've come to the end of this chapter, you will be able to identify your Fire Power. This is what you need to operate in your genius zone, where you can thrive at work. After completing the exercises in this chapter, you will have exciting, new ideas for potential opportunities and pathways to explore.

The Maverick Letters

Ruth Ramsay, adult sex educator

Dear reader,

I bent over and slowly slid my G-string down my thighs and calves, and over my high heels, as the final beats of a heavy rock track thumped out of the speakers above the stage. Straightening up, there I was: naked, in front of a room full of (mostly male) strangers, on a Wednesday afternoon, in a pub on the fringes of the City of London.

That was the pivotal moment in my career journey. Now I am an adult sex educator and coach, TEDx speaker and former award-winning striptease artist.

Soon after that audition in a striptease pub in 2002 (I got the job!), I left a blossoming career in fashion journalism. I'd had a fantasy of being a striptease artist since I was a child, but it wasn't something I could tell my parents or my school careers adviser. Instead, I had followed my other passion, journalism, hoping for a career in glossy magazines. I was on the road to that, but then I saw an advert for the London School of Striptease.

I took the school's beginners course, then the intermediate course, and a few weeks later was standing naked on that East End stage, feeling like I'd come home. Despite intense disapproval from my parents, boyfriend and friends, I became a stripper.

I've never regretted that decision. It led to over a decade of performing, teaching striptease, running events, modelling, doing activism around sexual rights, winning an erotic award and writing about sex. It was a euphoric glitter-and-sweat-soaked whirlwind.

In my late thirties, I left dancing to move out of London to be with my now husband and his kids. I worked as a personal fitness trainer while building a happy stepfamily, but I desperately missed the 'sexy world'… I did a life coaching diploma, not sure where it might lead, and then someone asked me to combine my life experience and new coaching skills to coach them around sex. Lightbulb moment!

Now I am three years into building a business as a sex coach, partly thanks to the viral success of a TEDx talk I did in 2023 ('Revamp your sex life in six minutes'), which has had over 1.5 million views. I run busy courses and webinars, have a full roster of one-to-one clients, and still regularly indulge my passion for striptease by teaching it. I love my work and find it endlessly fascinating and rewarding.

On one hand, my step out of the mainstream publishing world and onto the stage was easy, as I felt such an intense pull towards it; but I faced lots of criticism and negativity. I was told I would 'never get a proper job after this', 'never be respected by any man again', and – most upsetting of all – that I was 'personally responsible for the abuse of women and girls in this world'. I lost my boyfriend, some friends and, for a few months, my relationship with my parents. However, I felt in my heart I was doing something good and right, and my life experience has since proved that.

It was also scary, to step out of the safety of an employed job into something entirely unreliable with zero job security or rights. When you are acting from your true heart, though, you have focus, energy and bravery. Fast-forward 20 years, and I still have that: while struggling to build my coaching business, I did low-brainpower casual work, wanting my head full only of my business. I rehearsed my TEDx talk again and again while cleaning toilets at a local Airbnb.

Where's the lesson for you in this? Trust your instinct, follow the path you know is right for you, and work hard for as long as it takes.

If you're struggling to know your life's purpose, ask yourself, Who am I in my daydreams? I fantasied about being a striptease artist for 15 years or so before it happened. That person you think of as your fantasy alter ego might actually be your true self. What would happen if you gave them more space in your life? Why are you afraid to do so?

Read The Crossroads of Should and Must *by Ella Luna and inspirational books such as the one you are holding in your hands right now. Have life coaching with a coach specialised in helping clients discover their purpose – it could be the best investment in your wellbeing you ever make.*

What if you already know your purpose? If you've felt it right from when you were a child, but have never explored it? Then I urge you to do so, however bizarre it may seem. Even if it means getting naked in a roomful of strangers on a Wednesday afternoon.

Good luck.

Ruth
www.ruthramsay.com

Christian Amys, Urban Forage

Dear forager,

In 2002 I moved to France to start a gap year, which turned into multiple gap years. I became a semi-professional athlete, competing in French snowboard competitions. To make ends meet, I would wash dishes, work on bar doors and collect glasses.

I realised I was a really good cook and worked well under pressure, so I trained as a chef or cuisinier, travelling from the French Alps to the southwest coast and the Basque

Country. Returning to the UK in 2011, I worked in some of the best restaurants in the UK. After appearing on BBC1's MasterChef: The professionals *(I was a Quarter Finalist in 2019), running my own restaurant and expediting Michelin food, I lost my job in the first Covid lockdown.*

While attempting to isolate, I began a journey through the Sussex countryside, foraging every day and documenting my finds on social media. Soon I was supplying wild food to vulnerable people; finding rare, forageable produce for chefs; and constantly being asked, 'Take us foraging.' I spent the rest of isolation planning how I could make this into a living.

I now run forage workshops, where we teach anyone how to identify and harvest wild food. I also supply a handful of bespoke clients and make our own foraged products. I have always been a do-what-I-want kind of person so always followed my dreams, but I have always tried to be authentic and make a real difference in whatever I turn my hand to.

When I set up Urban Forage, I wanted to create a community where we could all share our love of foraging and do it in the safest, most respectful way, and to encourage more people into the hobby. Some of the biggest challenges I've faced are due to my health – I've always struggled with diabetes and have a number of mental health conditions. These were very difficult to manage as a chef, which is why it was even more important to create a career that would allow me more time for self-care. I've always struggled for money, and after putting all my savings into a kitchen (investments that I never saw back), I set up my current business with no money and on Universal Credit (which I am still on). I've never focused on making money, because if you make a good enough product that represents fair value, you can always survive.

Now I am able to spend my days planning, foraging, eating, living and providing the most incredible experiences for my clients. I sleep well at night, and the best reward is the amazing reception we get on our forage experience days. I am slowly but surely reaching a stage of alignment with being comfortable in what I do and make and, as a result of my health improving, am able to focus and deliver even better results.

I would advise you to follow your dreams and, if you have a realistic goal, focus on that. Anything can be achieved with some hard work. I would recommend planning your venture as much as you can – business plans, financial forecasts and market research were important for me to gauge if my project was achievable. If I was to do it all over again, I would probably slow down and try to do less, to focus on what's in front of me more.

Good ideas can only be good if they are executed. Plan what you want to do, and then work out how the hell you will get there and what you need.

Keep on truckin'.

Christian
www.urbanforage.me

Five
Explore New Pathways

N ow that you know your values, vision and skills – your 'career compass' – it's time to calibrate that compass to map out your ideal job. While you may be excited by your newfound clarity, and it can be tempting to start applying for jobs, hold your horses.

Where to start

Often, my coaching clients have contacted recruitment agencies about their career change and cannot understand why they are not being met with excitement. The truth is that recruitment agents generally don't have huge salaries but are instead paid in commission if they meet their monthly targets. It is not in their interest to have a candidate who does not possess the skills or experience of the job brief given to them by their client. It is rare to come across a recruitment agent who sees the potential in a client, goes out on a limb, and convinces their client to interview a candidate seeking a career change that only meets part or a small percentage of the brief.

Thinking of this from the other side: most companies have an inhouse recruitment team, who will already have discussed the skills and experience required to do the job and where the flex is. Some jobs are technical and require a level of expertise. If the inhouse recruitment team are unable to source such a person, they may engage a recruitment agency that specialises in that specific industry. If the company is prepared to pay a fee to the recruitment agency, they will want a candidate who meets the requirements of the role. In other words, they want bang for their buck; or as I refer to it, the moon on a stick.

Recruitment agents might only get to work on one to three vacancies per month, while the rest of their time is spent on new business development, finding companies to sign up and work with them. They will therefore rarely spend time giving career change advice. It can help to think of them as sales agents – they are external to the business they are recruiting for so won't have knowledge of the inner working of the business, the culture, succession gaps or pain points.

Instead of relying on recruitment agencies, focus on connecting with people in the space you are interested in working in, or with people who are living the lifestyle you want. Most of the projects I have worked on came through connecting directly with relevant people. When you are considering a career change, connecting with the right people is a more effective approach than going through recruitment agencies.

Brave new worlds

Often, when clients come to me, they have been so paralysed by the fear of trying something new and getting it wrong that they have remained comfortably uncomfortable.

I share this thought with those clients...

Imagine you're at a crossroads in a maze, and each path is shrouded in mystery. You're hesitant to choose a path because you fear making the wrong decision. However, if you stay rooted in place, you'll remain lost in the labyrinth. If you dare to pick a direction, even if it initially seems wrong, you have the opportunity to adjust your course and eventually find your way out. The key is to take that first step – indecision will only prolong your journey. Just take one step forward, and you will be better off for it. It's better to act these things out than to spend time trying to figure them out without taking action.

You will need to research different jobs that may be of interest to you. Don't rush this stage. Give yourself permission to experiment and embrace new learnings, and enjoy the process of discovering new avenues. This is a wonderful gift to give yourself – an opportunity to explore and find enjoyment in new or forgotten hobbies or skills. Try stepping into different worlds, sparking fresh ideas. At the same time, you will be crossing off things that don't work for you rather than leaving them as open questions in your mind. This process doesn't need to be daunting, and there are no limits to the opportunities it may lead to.

EXERCISE: Exploring new opportunities

Think about your energy audit from Chapter One and your vision board from Chapter Three. Evaluate where you are spending most of your time:

- What gets you fired up?
- What are you passionate about?
- What do you get so engrossed in that time flies by?
- Is there anything you regret not doing?

This doesn't have to be about a career; it might be related to a hobby – perhaps something that brought you joy when you were a child.

Jot down a mind map on a piece of paper and add anything and everything you would like to try.

Over the next three days after this exercise, research any local or online groups you can participate in. Meetup can be a good online resource, as well as local colleges or news boards.

Before committing to a course, consider joining a taster session. What is the worst that could happen? Maybe it won't lead you to your next job, but you will have tried a new avenue and ticked it off your list. A great outcome would be that you enjoyed it, met interesting people with a shared interest, perhaps making a friend. It may at least have sparked an idea for something else. Keep in mind that you can now enjoy focusing on what's important in your life. It's time you prioritised yourself.

I love art and have an eclectic palette; I love nothing more than a mooch around the Brighton Lanes, drifting in and out of art galleries. I'm obsessed with Moorish architecture and have a coffee table full of art books. I'm not particularly good at painting, but it gives me escapism, stills my mind and allows me to be present. I find the process calming. Your hobby could become your next business idea. According to a 2021 report by the insurance company Aviva, 10.8 million UK adults plan to add to their incomes or make a full-time career from a hobby.

ARTISTIC FREEDOM

Naomi Wallens quit her corporate job making toys to pursue a career as a sculptor and, as an act of rebellion, 'found her freedom' making artwork from casts of her bottom. At 44 years of age, Naomi exhibited her art at Saatchi.

'I followed a pre-conditioned journey through school into university and into the corporate world to follow a "successful" path, and when I got there, I realised how desperately unhappy I had become,' she says. 'Living for the weekend, living a life that was successful in the eyes of society but painful in my heart and unfulfilling and meaningless to my soul. My light started to go out. I didn't make a decision to go into art, but in the depths of my unhappiness, I just started to paint again.'

The 30-day challenge

Approach this with your values, vision and strengths – your career compass – in mind. Think of the challenge as an information-gathering experiment. Keep an open mind and see it as an opportunity to explore and experiment, as play rather than a chore. You never know when you may make a new contact, or when a conversation may lead you to an interesting opportunity.

Informational interviews

Contacting people who do the job that interests you can be a valuable way to learn from their experiences, including their daily activities and transferable skills. It can also be a great way to network and secure a mentor working in that field. LinkedIn is a good resource for finding people to contact. If you don't know anyone in that specific field, put a call out on social media: *Does anyone know someone who works in [field]?*

Do your homework and look at any new contacts' LinkedIn pages and other social media or websites associated with them. Be mindful of people's time. It's likely they will be professionally busy, so sometimes a Zoom call is more convenient for them. If you are meeting in person, buy them a coffee. Offer up something in return such an interesting webinar related to their industry or to an interest of theirs.

Make sure you are on time for the call or meeting and have sensible questions prepared, to ensure you use the time wisely. Start with the easy questions:

- Why did they choose that industry?
- What parts of the job do they love?
- What were some of the challenges they faced when transitioning from one career to the next?

Once the conversation is flowing, you can move onto the more challenging questions:

- What's the pay really like?
- Is it even possible for someone to move into that field with no experience?
- Would you have to retrain?

- How long will it take to make your way back up the career ladder?

- What else might you need to consider?

Role models

Think about people whose lifestyle you want – even the ones you envy and feel jealous of. Deep down, it's less about being jealous of the person and more that you desire their lifestyle, and that's OK.

Reach out to them and tell them you admire what they have achieved and that you are considering a career move. Ask if they would be open to speaking with you for 30 minutes to explain how they got to where they are.

Again, make sure you are on time for the call or meeting and have sensible questions prepared, to ensure you use the time wisely.

Trade shows and networking events

Attend industry-related events, conferences, workshops or webinars to connect with professionals and gain a broader understanding of different career paths. When I was writing this book, I would pose questions to my networking group, which would often lead to an introduction. Usually, that precipitated a call or meeting, and something amazing would come out of the encounter.

This is how I met most of the people who have shared their inspiring stories in this book. Some of these individuals have become friends; others have featured me on their podcasts or YouTube channels, or invited me to retreats and workshops. These connections have led to speaking engagements and other collaborations – a wonderful ripple effect.

Professional associations

Often, professional associations' websites offer useful resources, networking opportunities, events and members you could contact. You may want to join a local group such as the Chamber of Commerce, which is a fantastic source of information; or Enterprise Nation, which supports small businesses.

Volunteering or internships

Think back to high school, when you completed two weeks of work experience, which gave you an insight into the job role. If anything, my work experience at least taught me I didn't want to go into interior design.

Volunteering and internships can be great ways of gaining hands-on experience, helping you determine if the job could be a potential new career path.

Online portals

Explore job listings on platforms like LinkedIn, Indeed, Glassdoor and Monster to understand job descriptions, including the required skills and qualifications, and the compensation for different roles.

Podcasts and books

These can be a wealth of information about specific industries, job roles and market trends. Don't be shy – simply reach out to podcast hosts, interviewers or authors.

Back in 2017, I read *The Escape Manifesto* by the founders of Escape the City (www.escapethecity.org), Rob Symington, Dom Jackman and Mikey Howe. I felt inspired by these like-minded individuals. They were running breakfast meetings a few streets from where I was working, so I signed up. Through their programmes, I met Sallee Poinsette-Nash, founder of Brandable & Co. (www.brandableandco.com); Marc Figueras, co-founder of Nest (www.keynest.com); and Pip Murray from Pip & Nut (www.pipandnut. com); and I was mentored by Ed Smith, co-founder of Doisy and Dam (https://balance.media/ founder-focus-doisy-and-dam). You never know what listening to a podcast or reading a book could lead to.

Friends and family

I guarantee that even if someone within your immediate network isn't in the field you are interested in, they more than likely know someone who is – a neighbour's son or niece, a best friend or a cousin of an in-law. Reach out to everyone you know to find out if they have contacts who are involved in the new career path you're considering.

Finding your motivation

When our career aligns with our interests, we experience a range of benefits, including some of the following:

- Work no longer feels a momentous chore but gives us joy and motivation.

- A career based on our passions can significantly enhance our wellbeing and work–life balance.

- Our newfound, intrinsic motivation propels us towards achieving our goals and overcoming obstacles, and gives us a sense of satisfaction.

- Perpetual learning challenges us to step outside our comfort zone and grow, cultivates creative thinking and sparks innovative solutions. It keeps our mind active and receptive to new skills and knowledge.

- Creativity flourishes when we love what we do, and it allows us to be authentic and true to ourselves. This can be an empowering and liberating experience.

LIFE'S A BEACH

Jessie Tuckman quit her job as a loan and mortgage broker in Manchester to move to Cornwall, to pursue her passion for surfing and become a topflight surfer and sports model.

She competes regularly and loves every minute. She says surfing has changed her life and introduced her to new people, places and experiences.

CRAFTING A NEW CAREER

During lockdown, Emma Eatwell monetised her newfound hobby, which became a business.

'I stumbled upon a resin kit my sister had gifted me years before. Bored, I decided to open it up. By combining pressed flowers and leaves with resin, I found an incredible sense of joy and purpose in creating. I began crafting unique gifts that carried deep meanings. Flowers, after all, have their own meanings, and I used them to convey messages of love, remembrance and good luck. It wasn't long before these creations became more than just beautiful objects – they became heartfelt tokens of connection during a time when physical distance was our reality.

As demand increased, I knew I had to turn my side hustle into something bigger. I registered Cotswold Crafts by Emma in September 2020. By October, I had begun selling on Amazon. What happened next is something I'd never have guessed. Soon, that £20 resin kit from my sister would lead to a turnover of over £100,000. Looking back, the one thing I would advise my younger self would be to have the confidence to start this whole creative journey earlier in my career.'

It's a goal!

Imagine, 12 months from now, that you are living the dream. You have attained the lifestyle and career that you desire, and you are doing things that bring you joy and possibility. How does it make you feel?

Now that you have awareness of your career compass, Fire Power and skills gaps, the following exercise will help you to make your goals a reality.

EXERCISE: Let's make this happen

Revisit your vision board.

Think about your goals – what you need to do to make your dreams happen. Break those goals down into short-, medium- and long-term goals. Each goal needs to be SMART: specific, measurable, achievable, relevant and time-bound. List them on a sheet, creating something like the list outlined below.

Break the short-term goal down by working out the actions you need to take in the next 90 days towards your overall short-term goal, separating the actions by month. Next to each goal, list three action steps you will need to take to achieve your monthly goal, including a deadline for each action step.

Repeat step 3 for your medium- and long-term goals so that you have a clear plan of everything you need to do over the next 12 months.

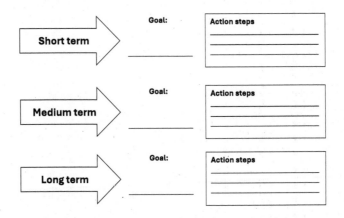

For example, if you are working in marketing and want to transition into freelancing in 12 months' time, you will need to find clients. You might decide initially to advertise your services on Upwork, to obtain client testimonials and create a portfolio of work. You need a website and relevant social media pages to promote your services.

You decide your three main goals are obtaining clients, creating a website and promoting your business on social media. You decide to break them down into smaller aims, setting deadlines to complete each goal by month four, month eight and month twelve, respectively. You are now able to list next to each of the three goals what actions you need to take to launch your business in a year's time. For the website, your first action might be researching the best platforms, registering your domain and setting up your email address. Second, you need to write the content and take professional photo images of you and your work. Third, you may want to get some friends to test each web page for feedback before promoting it.

Here are some important factors to bear in mind while you plan your first 12 months.

- **Daily actions:** After you have completed the exercise above, break it down to daily actionable steps. To stay committed to reaching your goals, it is important to keep taking action, however small. Jack Canfield talks about the Rule of Five concept in his book *The Success Principles*. To meet your goal, Canfield says you need to think about what five actions you need to take each day. For example, to build a following on social media, you might want to post a blog, reply to a direct message, comment on a prospective customer's post, send an email and post a short video.

- **Accountability:** Define how you'll hold yourself accountable for taking action on your plan. Will you regularly check in with a mentor, coach or accountability partner? Perhaps you want to share your vision and action plan with a trusted mentor and seek their feedback and insights.

- **Flexibility:** By embracing the principles of SMART goals and breaking your objectives down into manageable tasks, you lay the groundwork for meaningful progress. However, amid the hustle and bustle of pursuing your goals, don't overlook the importance of flexibility and adaptability. This includes periodically revisiting your vision, which may evolve over time. The journey to a career change is rarely linear, and being open to adjusting your course ensures you can navigate unexpected challenges with resilience and grace.

- **Reflection:** Regular self-reflection is key – an opportunity to pause, assess your progress and fine-tune your approach. Don't forget to celebrate the milestones along the way, no matter how small. Each achievement is a testament to your dedication and a reminder of how far you've come. The important thing is to keep moving forward to your end goal. As your vision begins to take shape, remember that this is just the beginning – a prelude to the detailed planning and execution I will cover in Part Three.

Summary

This chapter has given you practical tips on how to research the new career avenues you want to explore and on how to start building your network. When you have identified your new direction in life, it's vital to have the courage to start to make things happen, which requires self-motivation and careful planning. Once you have your 12-month action plan laid out, and you build in other factors such as accountability and flexibility, you will be a big step closer to making your dreams a reality.

The Maverick Letters

Adam Moseley, Tamp & Grind

Dear entrepreneur,

I'm 37 years old, and have spent the last 19 years working full-time as a firefighter in Sussex, Hampshire and, most recently, London. I have always had a keen interest in building businesses, and I definitely have entrepreneurship coursing through my veins. Tamp & Grind – a specialty coffee shop in Lancing, West Sussex – is actually my third business. Most firefighters run side hustles alongside their shifts, because the pay in the public sector is pretty poor.

I sold my window cleaning business for a very good price in 2022, then bought a little Piaggio Ape tuk-tuk mobile coffee shop for my new side hustle. I had been passionate about coffee for about 15 years, but it had never been more than a hobby. I researched my pitch, setup costs, permissions, etc, before buying and getting the ball rolling.

I started the business in November, and anyone that knows the British winter will know it's not for the faint-hearted. It truly was a test of my determination and grit to stand outside for six or so hours in torrential downpours, -2°C temperatures, on some days with 50–60 mph gusting winds.

I fell in love with the concept and mostly earning money for doing two things I absolutely love – making coffee and conversations. They always say to do something you love for work, and you'll never work another day in your life; I've got to say that resonates with me immeasurably.

The company whose forecourt I parked the tuk-tuk on for nearly a year saw my determination and invited me to go into partnership with them to open my first coffee shop. We worked out all the financials and – basically – we did it, opening my first shop in October 2023.

A friend of mine asked what my USP is for my coffee shop – what do I offer that is unique? Well, at first, I didn't have a clear answer for this. Over time, though, I have realised two things my shop offers that are unique:

1. *Passion shines through the product. I get told time and time again the coffee I serve is amazing. It is, I agree (but it can always be better!).*

2. *My team and I make people feel welcome, even if it's just asking how their day is going. It's so simple, yet nearly no other coffee shop or hospitality business takes the time to actually show real interest in their customers.*

The turning point to leaving my 19-year career (which I had planned to retire in) was when I realised how much more fulfilled I felt creating my own path, not following one laid out by the local government world. I get to choose when, how and what I do for work. I literally get to make all the decisions and call all the shots. Some things don't work, and some things work amazingly; but either way, it's all about learning, and it's what makes it all so unique and exciting.

My current venture gives me a real sense of purpose. I feel that if I have to shut for a day or reduce hours of the shop that I'm actually letting customers down that rely on their little five-minute window each morning to stop in and have a moment of calm and a meaningful conversation, along with a damn fine coffee.

I think luck doesn't exist in the form most people think of it, and that it's something we make ourselves. You have to take risks and chances in life. These risks and chances don't have to be reckless – they can be calculated, and you can have checks in place in case something isn't paying off – you can try plan B or plan C.

If you have something you're really interested in or passionate about, then I have absolutely no doubt you can make a living from doing it (and get even better at it in the process). We really do only get one shot in life. The only thing that's certain is that none of us are getting out of here alive, so make your time on earth count. Fulfil your dreams and passions.

I have built so many relationships in the last 12 months with other coffee entrepreneurs. Many have dipped their toe into running their own businesses but haven't fully leapt out of their full-time employment yet. My advice would be to do your passion on the side of your full-time job, if possible; or reduce your full-time hours (drop one day a week), then you can put some serious time and effort into your new venture without too much risk.

I don't have any specific quotes that have guided my career, other than You cannot rush perfection, *which is proudly presented in my coffee shop. I would, however, say I've always believed in investing in good equipment. I always promised myself a brand new La Marzocco Linea coffee machine for my first coffee shop, which is a whopping £12,500 on its own – nearly half of our budget for the full fitout of the coffee shop. Was it worth it? Absolutely. I get comments every day on how awesome the coffee machine looks (and it is an absolute workhorse).*

Just remember: talk is cheap. For every person that encourages you and says it will all be amazing, you'll get 10 that know better and tell you there's no way you'll be successful.

Just do your due diligence. Are these people successful or have they been in dead-end jobs for 30 years? You may not always know best, but you'll often know better!

Adam
www.tampgrind.co.uk

PART THREE
YOUR ESCAPE PLAN

Six
Find Your Squad

When it comes to a career change, moving into freelancing or starting a business, I cannot over-stress the importance of finding your community of cheerleaders – your *squad*. As much as friends and family are great, they won't always understand your dream. When I decided to do a master's degree in my thirties, with the intention of changing career, it was met with resistance from my parents in the form of questions:

- Why are you doing another degree?

- Why don't you stick to the career you have?

- Is this going to hold you back from progressing up the career ladder?

- Can you afford the student loan?

- Are you going to be able to pay your bills?

These questions were rooted in fear. *Their* fear.

It was 2008, and the economy had taken a dive. I'd been working in the hospitality trade and was itching to do something new. My role had evolved from being a manager into visiting sites to investigate why they were under-performing. It was exciting but by no means glamorous. Often, it meant living out of a suitcase, staying in budget hotels and eating out of vending machines. The role inevitably meant performance-managing people out and replacing them, which became a thankless task – needless to say, I would be met with distrust and suspicion from the staff. It did pique my interest in a career in human resources, though.

Unfortunately, the economic downturn meant the market was competitive and companies could be selective. I knew a master's degree would set me apart from the competition. I also knew I couldn't afford to study full-time. I therefore applied for a student loan and studied two years part-time while working full-time. It was tough, but it helped me to transition into a new career.

Fortunately, my fellow students were also working full-time, albeit with their employers sponsoring them. When the chips were down, they would rally around and cheerlead me on.

I did the same when I was creating my coaching practice, and again when I started writing this book – I surrounded myself with like-minded people on a similar journey. Some of those people had already published a book or had been running their business for several years.

Do not underestimate the power of advice and support. If you want to overcome your fears and the self-doubt associated with starting a new career, you are going to need to talk to people who have successfully managed a career change. Like the Mavericks in this book, those people will give you a realistic perspective on the difficulties surrounding the endeavour, but they will also help you believe it is possible.

The power of community

From a 2017 *Business Insider* report, according to author and entrepreneur Tim Ferriss, 'You are the average of the five people you most associate with.' His association with different people ebbs and flows, depending on what he's working on and trying to achieve. In other words: if you want your own business, find a networking group of founders – surround yourself with people who have done the same.

Researching networking groups might be a matter of trial and error until you find the one where you connect with people on a journey similar to yours. It will help to consider some questions:

- Does the purpose of the group closely align with your goals?

- What is the group's values?

- Does the group regularly meet and how structured is the meeting?

- Does it offer both in-person meetings and online meetings? (Both can be beneficial depending how constrained you are for time.)

When I moved from London to the Sussex coast, I struggled to meet people. I relocated in 2019, and eight months later we went into lockdown. As happened for many people, my job role became remote. Although I spent time in coworking spaces and coffee shops, I still found it difficult to make meaningful connections.

I am an introvert, which means I get overwhelmed being around lots of people, and I find myself retreating and becoming socially awkward. Instead, I get my energy from smaller groups. Consider your style, because this is an important factor when selecting a networking group and the value you will gain from it.

It wasn't until I joined Found & Flourish, founded by Lara Sheldrake (whose story is in this book) that I found my squad. Lara, like me, had moved from London to Brighton and then to West Sussex, and she has been an amazing cheerleader for me from the get-go. She set up Found & Flourish to create a community connecting and inspiring founders and free-lancers. Everyone in that community was welcoming and seemed genuinely excited to learn more about my business.

When I decided to write this book and told members of the group at the regular Hugs and Brunch event hosted by Lara, my announcement was met with enthusiasm and interest. Instead of fear, doubts or questions about why I would do it, members were interested, asked plenty of questions and volunteered ideas. They became a great resource, and everyone in the group has followed my journey and celebrated each milestone with me. Inevitably, someone knew an editor, a copywriter, an illustrator or a graphic designer – anyone I needed to help me succeed. On the day that I told the group, I left brunch feeling like an author; suddenly the idea of writing a book seemed possible.

An important piece of advice, which Lara will attest to, is that you mustn't underestimate the power of community. They say it takes a village to raise a child, and I am convinced it takes a community to create a business. My squad has saved me in time, mistakes and potential costs. I have sometimes spent hours researching the best sales funnel or platform, reading through endless blogs about pros and cons, weighing up the cost versus the value. Then, when I have admitted defeat and posed the challenge to my squad, they've immediately sent practical responses and recommended tried and tested solutions.

Most networking groups – whether local or online groups – offer a free trial or the ability to cancel without a long-term commitment. I would recommend starting with your immediate network, or contacting someone via social media who is running a business in the industry you are interested in getting into, for recommendations on networking groups. If you cannot find the group you are looking for, you can create one on Meetup.

When you find your squad, they will energise you, motivate you and lift you up when you are down. Don't forget to make sure you reciprocate by providing value to your community whenever you can.

Testing the great escape

I have been a member of plenty of online groups at various times throughout my career. Some have been industry-related groups, while others have been related to money, PR, social media, podcasting or fitness. Membership often includes webinars, access to a private community, discounted courses, and tips and advice, for which you pay a monthly fee. They can be a useful source of information and a great way to obtain feedback about your business ideas. Many of them run promotional membership discounts throughout the year. They can also be a great way to beta-test a product you have created.

Back in 2018, when I joined Escape the City after reading their book, I was yearning to get out of the rat race and move away from London. I had just read Tim Ferriss's book, *The 4-Hour Work Week*, and was hungry for a group of like-minded people. I dragged a colleague along to the Motivational Mondays sessions they ran before work. The room was filled with about 20 individuals, of all ages and backgrounds, who wanted to escape the corporate life and create something on their own terms. The energy in the room was electric. I was pumped.

The session ended with hugging the person next to you, much to my colleague's horror – she is even more introverted than me and the least tactile person I know. Paradoxically, that day didn't only have a positive impact on me. It set the wheels in motion for my colleague, who booked a month's trip to South America, started her own online business, and then quit her job and moved to Ireland.

Escape the City is still going strong, and ironically, they too escaped London. These days they run their office in Brighton, and the company has evolved into an online jobs board, advertising interesting jobs to work with cool startups. They are a great resource and taught me a lot about starting a business on a budget.

Apart from moral support, the other benefits of having a squad are:

- Profile-raising

- Finding referral partners

- Receiving business advice

- Identifying personal solutions

- Increasing collaboration

- Improving business development

- Sourcing supplier recommendations

- Building self-confidence

- Expanding knowledge

- Upskilling

- Strengthening personal development

Forming bonds – including lasting friendships – also improves your mental and physical health. According to an article by Christopher Bergland for *Psychology Today*, studies show that as you build relationships, you establish a sense of self-worth and value, and strong social ties may reduce stress and heart related illness. Providing advice to others and helping them succeed can give you an emotional boost.

I would recommend establishing a trusted circle – a sounding board. Mine is a group of about 10 people from different backgrounds, in consulting, coaching, tech, design, ecommerce and marketing. Most of them are founders. I don't pay for their services, and they don't pay for mine. Instead, we share ideas and problem-solve. They are brutally honest and will tell me if something sucks; and that's OK, because it helps me to develop the idea and create something better.

I do not recommend having family as your sounding board. They will often tell you something is great to avoid hurting your feelings, which won't help you. Or, worse still, they won't fully understand your new idea. Instead, they will give you every reason under the sun why you shouldn't proceed, suck the life out of your idea and demoralise you.

Tapping into wisdom

Getting a mentor – someone who has the benefit of wisdom, and ideally someone you can contact regularly – is a smart move. Unlike coaches, mentors are directive and will impart their advice. If you are lucky enough to know someone who is happy to mentor you for free, seize that opportunity.

I have been fortunate to have mentors at different times of my life. One mentor who stands out is Guy Welply, who was my boss when I was working in the bar trade. He taught the managers there a lot about business and the importance of teamwork. He took no prisoners, but he also gave credit where it was due. As managers, we loved and loathed Monday mornings, when we had our weekly management conference call to go through the end-of-week numbers. We certainly made sure we came to that call knowing our sales, overheads, gross and net profit figures.

To this day, I have never worked for another leader like Guy. He understood how to empower his team and instil accountability and camaraderie. It's the only team I have been part of where colleagues would actively volunteer to give up their night off to cover colleagues' shifts, or rally round and pull shifts behind the bar when it was short-staffed. Whether Guy realises it or not, he created a squad. Incidentally, he escaped the rat race in 2006 to take a career break diving in Thailand… and never returned. He now owns a luxury boutique villa in Koh Tao.

It's worth paying for a mentor if you can afford it. I would recommend a referral from someone you trust, who you know has good connections. Be selective and pick someone who has run or is still successfully running businesses and not only has strong experience but is well respected. Do your homework. There are plenty of folk claiming to be seven-figure business owners. They may have flashy websites, have tonnes of followers across every social media platform, and always appear to be off to a tropical destination, wrapped around an expensive car or sitting in a jet. Anyone can take a selfie in front of someone else's Ferrari outside Harrods, though, or pay to sit in a jet or a plush penthouse for 20 minutes. CGI can also make the bleakest places look tropical. Don't believe everything you see on social media.

Also consider having a coach. A good coach is worth their weight in gold and will pay for themselves ten times over, based on the results they help you achieve. Unlike mentors, coaches are non-directive. They won't give you the answers, but they will ask you powerful questions to help you arrive at the answers you need.

I have had a health coach, a mindset coach, a business coach, a writing coach and an accountability coach. Some coaches will provide a blend of coaching and mentoring, depending on your expectations. Carefully select a qualified coach with expertise in the topic you are focusing on – unfortunately, there are plenty of people claiming to be a coach who have had zero formal training. Remember too: you get what you pay for.

Staying accountable

It can be useful to have an accountability partner, who you can trust to keep you grounded and on track, and motivated to reach your goals. When I am working on a specific project that requires my focus and momentum, I have a weekly call with my friend, Jenny Braithwaite, who happens to be a business coach. Jenny can help point out areas I have overlooked and offer a different perspective, helping me to address any blind spots.

My relationship with Jenny offers mutual support, encouragement and feedback, which has created a support system to help me navigate obstacles. If I am struggling to hit a deadline, it's usually because the task is a heavy lift or I'm struggling to decide between several options, which can end up in analysis paralysis. Being able to chat through challenges with an accountability partner, and using them as a trusted sounding board, helps maintain productivity and momentum.

Summary

This chapter has been about the importance of surrounding yourself with the people who will make you successful, including those who have taken similar journeys. It has explained how you can find or create the networking group you need. A community of like-minded people, and a mentor or coach, will help you to reach your full potential. A trusted circle of friends will allow you to share ideas and problem-solve with others, and an accountability partner will help keep you grounded and motivated.

The Maverick Letters

Lara Sheldrake, Found & Flourish

Dear founder,

I left recruitment after finding myself getting wrapped up in not only the rat race but also the very male and toxic environment I found myself in working in. I loved the idea of helping people find their dream roles, but I ended up in a role where I was motivated by money over anything else. I lost myself in targets, incentives and financial success. At the end of the day, those weren't aligned with my values, and I got to the point where I didn't recognise who I was anymore.

I quit my role in recruitment before I knew what I wanted to do next, but I had got to a point of burnout. I took some time to heal and work out what it was that really fed my ambition and felt like my Ikigai – my reason for being. I made a list of 10 things that were important to me, and I explored the concept of Ikigai. This gave me some time, space and creativity to work out what it was I wanted to do with my skills and passion.

I had always had a passion for social media, events and supporting businesses to raise their online profiles. I studied media and comms at university, then set up my first consultancy business when I left uni, but it never really took off. When I quit my role in recruitment, I applied for a few courses, started working with some early-stage founders, and built my experience from there. My mission was to work with impact-driven founders, and naturally, most of my clients were women. I loved what I did and worked on some really cool projects; I collaborated with a team of freelancers and had some great clients. I then got pregnant and took some time off to bring up my baby boy.

Three months later, I started getting itchy feet and wanted to get back to work. I realised that being thrown into a new role of motherhood was even more lonely than running my own business, and I knew I would struggle, so I went on the hunt for a community I could be a part of. I wanted access to resources and people who were ahead of me and had the insight I was lacking, and just to hang out with people who got it.

This was back in 2018, and I couldn't find anything that resonated. Then the idea of Found & Flourish was born.

I offer a community to women and nonbinary people braving the world of entrepreneurship. We provide a community of supportive people across the UK and Europe. We're mainly online so offer a variety of workshops, masterclasses and services to support founders. As well as this, we run localised events to keep people connected as we believe this is where the real magic happens.

Love,

Lara
www.foundflourish.co.uk

Karen Webber, Goodness Marketing

Dear square peg in a round hole,

I never thought I'd end up as a business owner.

Growing up, I wanted to be a writer. I was creative, and my world was a million miles removed from business owners, who I believed were all serious, stern and able to pull off a mean shoulder-pad look. Entrepreneurship was grey, and I was a rainbow.

A few decades later, and I was going up the management ranks in marketing. I was working hard and getting results for my employers and their clients. However, something was amiss. My working life lacked fulfilment, and what I did, day in and day out, felt at odds with who I am.

I mistakenly assumed the problem was me. Rainbows feel like they're the odd one out, if all around them they see grey.

I thought, 'Maybe I am not cut out for marketing.' I didn't want to trick or pressurise people into parting with their cash. I didn't want to manipulate people into making decisions that weren't going to serve them. I didn't want to fuel mindless consumption in the face of climate change.

My vision for marketing was different. I wanted marketing to empower people to make conscious decisions about buying. I wanted marketing to feel good, do good and get good results.

I felt completely alone, though – like I was the only one in the world with these unconventional ideas about marketing. I kept going, until the realisation of just how fleeting and precious time is hit me like a tonne of Lego (I had two young kids at this point).

Suddenly, it was crystal clear: I was spending so much of my precious time, skills and energy to advance something in which I didn't believe at all. I wasn't having the impact I wanted to have on the world, and I wasn't showing my kids what it was like to live a truly aligned life.

I knew that, even if I stood alone in my thoughts around marketing, I had to stand up for these beliefs and use my marketing powers for good. Something had to change. I wasn't in a position to dramatically quit my job, so instead I shuffled towards being able to do that. I negotiated part-time hours and secured a couple of freelance clients on the side. A few months later, I did take the (still uncertain) leap out of employment.

Of course, there were times where I longed for the security of a monthly pay cheque, but did I look back? Not really.

The biggest realisation of those early years of self-employment was that, no matter how unconventional your ideas or how seemingly unique your challenges, you are never, ever the only one. My squad had been out there all along. I soon realised that there were many others who shared my ideas about marketing and business, and also believed a better way is possible. There are existing communities, and there will always be someone ready to answer a question if you have the courage to ask.

Whether you're building a purpose-driven business or career, my best advice is to go and find your people. Trust me – it changes everything when you can walk the road less travelled alongside others.

The camaraderie and support of like-minded folk will sustain and inspire you as you carve out your version of a successful life. They will give you answers and new perspectives. Their support will lift you up when things feel tough. They'll inspire and sustain you and remind you why you have embarked on this heart-led journey.

So, dear square peg, this is my encouragement to let your rainbow shine bright, so the other rainbows know where to find you. When you embrace your uniqueness and surround yourself with those who see the world in technicolour, you'll find your pot of gold – no matter what your version of success looks like.

Know that in the world of purpose-driven work, you're never alone. There are others on the same-but-different journey, who can't wait to cheer you on. Go live your most authentic rainbow life.

I'm rooting for you.

With love,

Karen
www.goodnessmarketing.co.uk

Seven
Leverage Your Resources

Your dream might seem far away at this point, but believe it or not, you already have everything you need to make it happen. You only need to intentionally redirect your time and money.

If I had a pound for each time someone has told me they don't have time to create change in their life, or that money is a barrier, I would be very rich. Those obstacles can be overcome, step by step, like anything else. To make room for something new, though, such as your vision, you're going to have to let something go. You'll have to retrain some cherished habits, starting today.

Time

When I got serious about making a career change and needed time to experiment and upskill, I looked at my weekly pattern and realised there was an opportunity to leverage my time more effectively. All those nights watching Netflix were replaced with online courses; lunchtimes were spent on calls conducting informational interviews; and my commute was spent on research, reading books or listening to industry-related podcasts. Eventually, my evenings of online learning were replaced with:

- Creating my side hustle

- Working on my website

- Planning my social media posts

- Growing my email list

- Creating ebooks, online courses and programmes

When I was writing this book, I would wake up at 5 am and spend one hour focused on writing. I found my mind was clear, focused and creative, and it was uninterrupted time. Trying to write during my lunch break or in the evenings didn't work for me. In the middle of the day, my mind would inevitably be preoccupied by meetings I needed to prepare for, urgent emails I needed to respond to, or impending deadlines. By the time the evening came around, I would be drained, and my mind filled with the day's events and ruminating on the fires I would need to put out the following day.

At first, I found it hard to get up so early. However, after I had got into the routine, I started to enjoy it, as I felt more productive. Sometimes, by 8 am, I would have written a thousand words as well as clearing a laundry load, having breakfast and cleaning the kitchen. I then felt energised because I'd accomplished so much, and I'd had great thinking time while completing the chores.

You might be a night owl rather than an early bird, but you can structure your day to allow for uninterrupted creative time when it suits you best. Be disciplined about when you check emails or run errands. Tim Ferriss talks about checking emails twice a day – once in the morning and once before the end of the business day. At those times, he is fully focused on the emails and nothing else.

Close down pop-ups and any other sites to avoid becoming distracted during your work day. Give yourself a maximum of five minutes to skim through new emails in your inbox, deciding which ones to delete, delegate or do. Mark those that require urgent attention with a flag and action them as soon as possible. Those that are not so important or require some thought can be dealt with later in the week. Anything else can be deleted, delegated or filed away for reference.

Money

Financially speaking, a career change can be an over-whelming prospect at any age, but it can feel even more daunting as you get older. If you have already reached a higher career status, you might be the main breadwinner and responsible for your family's finances, and it is likely you will have more commitments and responsibilities such as a mortgage. Losing our livelihoods due to redundancy or career change is therefore more challenging.

In the *BBC Worklife* article 'Why Gen X isn't ready to leave the workforce', Sarah Blankenship, from Oklahoma in the US, says 'There is a major sense of urgency for Gen Xers. We often don't have the privilege of taking time off. A lot of Gen Xers – they're still behind on retirement. They are facing ageism in the workplace. Gen Xers still have families to support.'

Professor Michael S North agrees, 'Middle agers have more immediate pressures, on average, to earn an income, provide insurance for their families and the like.'

These factors can be compounded by financial stresses such as building a suitable pension for retirement and paying off a mortgage. As highlighted in a 2023 CNBC article, some data shows Gen Xers carry more debt burdens than other generations, and many of them are also part of the 'sandwich generation', providing for elderly parents and their own children.

We fall into the trap of telling ourselves that if we just earn more, we will have more time to spend on the things or the people we love, we'll be able afford a better lifestyle, and we can maybe eventually work less. I was guilty of this, convincing myself that if I got that promotion or applied for that new job with a pay rise, I would be able to pay off my debt and eventually work less or retire early. This wasn't true, though. Instead, a pay rise meant more responsibility, which inevitably meant longer hours and commuting distances. The fact is, it can be almost impossible to buy yourself out of debt, just as you cannot create more time by working.

I found myself leaving early for work and grabbing breakfast and coffee on the way to meetings. I would be too tired to cook in the evenings, instead ordering takeaways or having pre-made food delivered in bulk. I didn't have time to iron so would outsource it to the dry cleaners. If a shoe heel had broken, I would not have time to get it repaired and would buy a new pair of shoes on the way to the office. If something at home needed repairing, I'd book tradespeople regardless of the cost.

I was paying for convenience because I didn't have time, I didn't have time because I was working all hours, and I was working overtime to pay for a mortgage and bills. While I didn't have the biggest house on the street, I wanted to live in a nice and safe area which meant my budget was stretched.

Two books changed my mindset: Tim Ferris's *The 4-Hour Work Week*, and *The Millionaire Next Door* by Thomas J Stanley and William D Danko. Both books had a profound effect on me. I realised time had more value than money. I realised earning more wasn't going to change my lifestyle. Even those who win the lottery inevitably end up broke again because they splurge their wins on expensive items.

Budget review

I realised I needed to lower my outgoings, and I spent a weekend going through my finances and cancelling things like magazine subscriptions, old gym memberships and insurance for a laptop I no longer had. I looked at the largest outgoings – my mortgage and bills – and came up with ways of reducing these.

You can't escape the rat race if you keep burying yourself in deeper debt. Cut up your credit card and commit to buying only the essentials.

NEW PRIORITIES

My friend, Laura, loves shopping and buying beautiful things for her home and family. She was renowned for her elaborate and beautiful Christmas tree dressing, Halloween costumes and parties.

It wasn't until a family trip to Greece that she realised the long commutes and time away from home working meant she had missed out on her kids growing up. The only reason she'd taken a more senior role was to cover the costs of their lifestyle. Now she realised that her lifestyle focused more on things than on memories.

Returning home, Laura reviewed her family's finances, and three weeks later, she started to plan to reduce her working hours from full-time to part-time. 'I realised time is precious, it's irreplaceable, it's the one commodity you cannot buy. I was learning things about my kids on holiday that I had missed – things I was oblivious to – lost moments that I cannot get back. I made a decision there and then, while watching them play in the swimming pool, that I wanted to be more present in their lives, and nothing was more important.'

Reducing your expenses as much as possible will help you live within your means and save more money in the long term. Here are just a few ways you can start doing this now:

- Review your bills to switch to cheaper options where possible.

- Look through your grocery list for expensive items and things you don't need, for example, bottled water when you have tap water at home.

- Review direct debits for products or services you no longer use, especially old warranties and insurance plans.

- Draw up a budget. This should include an income column (which might include salary, inheritance, cash gifts, stocks, shares, pension, side hustle) and an overhead column (including mortgage or rent, bills, insurance, subscriptions, transport, food, private medical, vet bills). By seeing your total income and expenditure written down, you can calculate how much you are left to spend each month. You can also review each expense to determine where you can cut back and make reductions.

- Educate yourself about tax relief. I used to have no idea about gifting through surplus income, for example; and contributing to a pension and ISAs is an easy way to reduce your tax.

On top of all this, you can reinvest the money you've saved so you can grow it ten-fold in the long term, working towards attaining financial freedom.

Getting serious about saving

Many startups fail due to lack of capital. Ideally, you should try to have two years of salary in the bank so you can focus on the business and growth of your new venture. However, not everyone has the luxury of time to save up before exiting their job. Unexpected events such as redundancy, divorce or a death in the family may accelerate or delay your escape plan. You will need to adjust accordingly and, crucially, to continue to take action to maintain momentum.

If your business is struggling to succeed, it is always worth reviewing your income and outgoings and drawing up a budget plan. This can feel overwhelming if it's not something you regularly do or perhaps if money isn't something you and your partner talk about. Remind yourself that you can only move on from money fears by addressing them. My clients always feel better when they have a budget because they feel more in control. Go back and review your budget from earlier. If you skipped that section, I encourage you to revisit it now.

There are plenty of budget-planner templates out there to help you track your incomes and expenses. FIRE sites are a good place to start; otherwise, a simple Excel spreadsheet works well. Budget planning helps you to understand where you can make savings to create a buffer for your career change, for example, capital for retraining or for taking time off to focus on building the business.

If possible, have at least a slush fund (freedom fund) to cover six months of your basic living expenses, and try to avoid using it unless you experience a real emergency. Your freedom fund is to pay bills if your business takes longer than expected to take off, or if you have to take a pay cut to move into your new career. Of course, it can be a lot easier to raise a slush fund to cover living expenses if you are in a household with two incomes.

Home sense

As Robert Kiyosaki advises in his book *Rich Dad Poor Dad*, your home is a liability, not an asset, unless it is making you money. There are endless ways you can earn income from your home, with just a few illustrated in the stories below.

WELCOME VISITORS

When Kate was contemplating a move into freelancing, she worried about covering her mortgage. Rather than take in a lodger (she valued her space), she hosted foreign language students for a couple of weeks at a time.

'Most of the time they were at school during the day, which meant I could focus on client work uninterrupted. I even started to enjoy the company and learning from different cultures.'

CANINE COMPANY

When my friend, Sarah, left her corporate job in marketing to move into freelancing, she signed up with a company that puts dog owners in touch with local people who will take care of their pets while they are on holiday.

This meant Sarah could remain home freelancing while hosting a dog for a few days or weeks.

She says, 'Not only did I get the joy of looking after someone else's dog in my own home, but I could also focus on building my business, the extra money helped, and I ended up with regular dog clients.'

FINANCIAL SPACE

William needed to pay off his credit card debt, so he rented out his garage. He found his biggest customers were people giving up their tenancy to go travelling, who therefore needed dry and safe storage.

You can rent out just about any space – driveway, loft, basement, shed – as well as things such as your home or car, and even belongings such as designer bags.

BACK TO BASICS

When Ella split from her partner, she decided to move back home with her parents and let her house out to cover the mortgage and bills.

'Going through a separation was tough, but it made me reassess my life. I knew that I didn't want to remain working in the legal field. I've always had a creative side and decided to retrain as an interior designer,' she says. 'Moving back in with my parents was tough on my social life, but it gave me the space to make a career shift and set up my own business, which I am grateful for.'

LESS IS MORE

Sometimes, downsizing is the answer. Nigel and Lisa realised they didn't need a four-bedroom house so opted for a two-bed, which enabled them to pay off their mortgage.

The equity from the sale also freed up some cash, which allowed them to convert the garage into an annexe.

Letting their annexe to a lodger now generates a small income, of which half goes into a tax-free ISA account and the other half covers their bills.

INVESTING IN NATURE

When Mike's partner left, Mike was bought out of his share of their home, and he was in the fortunate position of not needing the extra cash. He realised he'd rather leave it to his kids but was dismayed to learn a big chunk would go towards inheritance tax.

Mike discovered that woodland wasn't subject to inheritance tax and so purchased a few acres. He also learned to coppice the land, which generated a small income, and he and his kids enjoyed camping in the woodland during the summer.

He says, 'Not only is the woodland an asset, which has gone up in value, it is something I can enjoy with my kids and know that one day they will be able to inherit it.'

Financial freedom

Escaping the rat race of course carries financial risks, and you will need to plan carefully before losing your corporate salary. Here are some helpful tips on ways you can plan to avoid financial issues:

Alternative budgeting

According to author and businessman George Clason, the secret to escaping the rat race is to pay yourself first instead of last. The average person tends first to pay their expenses such as rent, phone bills and internet charges, typically leaving them with very little disposable income, if any at all.

Instead, you should set aside a certain amount from your monthly salary to pay yourself first – maybe

£100 each pay period – then, with whatever is left over, you pay your expenses. If you fall short, you will be motivated to find a new stream of income to prevent you falling into debt. You might pick up a new side hustle such as freelancing, or get around to clearing out your wardrobe, loft or garage and sell items on eBay. Leverage your assets to make money for you and provide an additional income.

Essential groundwork

As you prepare to escape the rat race, it's important to save some backup funds. A lot can go wrong in the first few months, so you'll need:

- Capital that you can invest

- Cash for an emergency

- Money to support you in your transition

You should have at least six months of savings to cover your own salary after you take the leap. The best situation would be to have an asset making you money before you make your full transition. Sometimes, though, life hits you in the face with a curveball – maybe you or your partner experience a sudden job loss, and you're forced to scramble money together. If you find yourself in an emergency situation soon after your escape and don't have sufficient funds saved up, focusing on a freelance opportunity can help you get back on your feet in the interim.

The biggest mistake people often make is spending their savings in an emergency. You shouldn't *ever* dip into your savings – you need to let the process of compounding interest take its effect to build up a buffer. Consider opening a cash ISA, where the interest earned is tax free.

Investing for the future

You can't escape the rat race unless you invest your money in something that makes more money. You might invest in a new business, or in the stock market when stocks are affordable. You could invest in property, with a tenant paying the mortgage each month; if the property you purchased goes up in value, you can sell it for a profit in later years.

Another way to make a career change is by buying a franchise or existing business that is already proven to generate a profit.

Ultimately, you want to acquire assets that will make you money each month so you can earn a more scalable income. The assets you acquire could also lead to a big payday when you sell them. For instance, if your online store becomes highly profitable, you may choose to sell it for a higher price than you bought it for.

Keep in mind that there will always be risk involved. As reported in 2023 by UKBM, around 60% of UK businesses fail within their first three years. As we saw in the 2007 crash, again in the economic downturn in 2020, and with spiralling interest rates in 2023, the stock market sometimes crashes. Property also doesn't always go up in value. However, despite risk, there can be major rewards. When it comes to investment, start small. There are learning curves in business, stock markets and real estate investments. Before making a financial commitment, make an *educational* commitment. That way, you lower any financial risk during an economic downturn or during periods of uncertainty.

The people in my network who are financially stable are those with several income streams. If one income stream such as their job switches off, they have other income to keep them afloat. These people tend to be recession-proof. They aren't millionaires, but they proactively reduce their outgoings and find ways to make extra income. It also means they have the distinct advantage that if they don't like their boss, or no longer enjoy their job, they are in a financial position to make a change.

Passive income

Passive income is essentially about making money while you sleep. This is the opposite of active income, where you are trading your time for money – if you don't work, you don't earn.

Examples of passive income sources include:

- Online courses, ebooks and other digital products

- Dividends from investments, which are passive income and require little involvement from you

- Rental income

For semi-passive income, you could create YouTube videos until they become monetised and then add affiliate links to gain commission. This takes time and investment, though.

Thinking outside the box

I am not a qualified accountant or tax expert, and statutes change all the time, so please take time to do your own research. My point here, though, is that we often limit ourselves by making assumptions. If you are thinking about generating additional income or diversifying your assets as part of your escape plan, it is worth thinking laterally to understand the possibilities.

There is a method called FIRE: financial independence, retire early. Plenty of people are adopting money-saving strategies to enable them to retire in midlife so they can then focus on the things they enjoy. An example from a 2019 *The Guardian* article recounts how Alan Donegan achieved financial independence before 40 and is now in Los Angeles, pursuing his dream of screenwriting. With a £1 million investment portfolio, saved from consulting and a business school, he and his partner live without the need to work. They prioritise saving over spending, following the motto 'Buy your freedom first'. Alan stresses the importance of saving over escalating expenses, for example, by living in a modest flat and driving a practical car. Saving on a £15,000 income is tough but doable at £40,000, by adjusting lifestyle.

Interestingly, he claims high earners with lavish habits might find achieving financial independence more challenging. Despite sacrifices, the resulting freedom makes the journey worth it, though. 'I have the freedom to pursue my dream,' Donegan says.

Income generator

Here is a list of further suggestions:

- Renting out space, eg Stashbee, Peerspace
- Renting out a spare room, eg SpareRoom, Host Family Stay
- Dog walking
- Pet sitting
- Tutoring, eg TutorMe, Tutor.com, Studypool
- Selling an online course

- Selling an ebook

- Doing tasks for people, eg TaskRabbit

- Being a virtual assistant

- Getting paid to advertise on your car, eg Car Quids, Adverttu

- Selling your photos online, eg on Adobe Stock, Shutterstock, Fotomoto, Etsy

- Selling crafts or print on demand, eg on Etsy, Amazon, eBay

- Freelance writing, editing, graphic design, eg on Fiverr, FreeUp, Upwork

- Taking part in focus groups, eg Respondent.io, Focus4People

- Dividends from investments

- Short temping jobs, eg redwingwam

- Becoming a mystery shopper, eg Market Force

- Modelling

- Freelancing, eg Upwork, Fiverr

- Play games online, eg Swagbucks, InboxPoundsCar boot sales and eBay

- Cashback sites, eg OhMyDosh!

- Website testing, eg UserTesting

- Work as an extra, eg Extra People, Casting Collective

- Test products and services, eg TestingTime

- Paid survey sites, eg Testable Minds, Prolific

Other funding strategies

Perhaps the career you are intending to transition to offers government grants, loans or possibly angel investors. Potentially rewarding funding strategies can be found through the following:

- Enterprise Nation and Virgin Startup can provide a wealth of information.

- Your local Chamber of Commerce is likely to have a finance partner such as Barclays Bank, which runs programmes for startups.

- Crowdfunding can be an option, and there are plenty of platforms such as Kickstarter or GoFundMe.

- Crowdcube is an equity crowdfunding platform which connects founders with investors.

All of these have advantages and disadvantages, so it is worth doing your research. There are plenty of useful sources that can support startups, including:

- The British Library in London, which has information and free advice about setting up a business

- Local Enterprise Partnership and Business Support Helpline, which offers advice

- Research incubators and accelerator programmes

EXERCISE: Money mindset challenge

Draw up a spreadsheet listing your income and your overheads so you can see where cost savings can be made.

There will be some quick wins such as cancelling a magazine subscription or taking a flask of coffee to work. Even switching bank accounts can earn you money.

Think about maximising your pension contributions or shifting your savings to an ISA savings account and an ISA shares account. If you have exhausted those options, look at high-interest savings accounts.

This exercise doesn't have to be a chore. It can be fun to find more money towards your escape plan.

Summary

There's no need to give up on your vision because of lack of time or money. This chapter has included a wealth of ideas for maximising the potential of your existing resources to work in the service of your future plans, all with a view to achieving financial freedom.

The Maverick Letters

Abi Adams, Project Woman

Alright, you gorgeous human,

I don't think my younger self would quite believe the point I am currently at, and that it's all thanks to her. I hug her every day so she realises how much she is loved and appreciated. I've realised over the last few years how important looking after those little inner children really is to my communication, both internally and externally.

So, who the bloody hell am I? I ask myself that on a daily basis because, as a woman, I am constantly fluctuating between the many archetypes and emotional expressions my menstrual cycle development has educated, inspired and gifted me. As a foundation, and so you don't think I'm unhinged, hello. I am a speaker, mentor and the founder of Project Woman – the ultimate space of female health and expression for the 21st-century human.

When I didn't get to drama school after leaving secondary school, I mainly worked at my stepfamily's factory. Someone said I should go to beauty school, so my nan funded me the opportunity to study at Steiner on Maddox Street in London. It was understanding the body through massage that seriously got my attention, and it was this that took me on to study traditional Thai massage in Thailand, Greece and various places in the UK. I took a 10-year hiatus from this scene when I went to work in one of the top property companies in London, before starting up my own mobile organic spa, which served the extremely wealthy people (and a few celebs) of London Town. This then turned into an organic café, yoga and massage studio in my home in Woodford – effectively, I set up a commune in a Victorian terrace street.

My passion for understanding the body saw me live in India, Thailand and America, learning the art of yoga and yoga therapy, mixed movement and massage. I realised soon after that I was simply looking to understand all of the emotional baggage I had been carrying around with me and what I could do with it.

It was while I was in Miami, studying MMA, that I found my period! I had been menstruating since I was 14 and I had had my first child at this point. However, while doing 8–10 hours of movement a day, my bleed wasn't a waterfall of clots; I wasn't emotionally unhinged and there was no pain. When I returned, I fell into the rabbit hole of female health, which blew my mind. I realised just how little I knew of myself by not having a relationship with my menstrual cycle. I also got to see firsthand the manipulation, control and obscene amount of bias there was toward female health.

That was when I founded Project Woman. I believe there is another way a woman can experience her health, which enables her to feel her emotions within a safe space, which allows her to break through her own barriers to reveal the woman she was born to be. We do not have to endure, suffer, put up with and fight our way towards success when we are in the right environment. That environment is Project Woman.

The core values I carry within every ounce of my body are creativity, adventure and emotional expression. These actually bubble into and out of me through movement, music, art and nature. They are the pulse within my work and how I support others. I have to nurture these values within myself before I can support them in others – again, something I advocate to everyone.

If you're struggling to find your purpose, you're trying too hard. It's not that difficult. I remember the moment Project Woman was born. I was in a café in Soho, London, with my family, where I was reading the local magazine. There was an article on the wonderful charity Project Ø (they champion healthy seas and speak a lot about dead zones being a crisis point for the environment), and it hit me like a Central Line train. These dead zones PØ spoke of reminded me of a woman's womb, through the lack of support, education and emotional expression we had towards them. It was so easy, I could have flippantly dismissed it (because it has to be hard, right?). However, every cell in my body kept on reminding me of Project Woman, and four years later, great things are happening and the tide is turning.

The only real obstacles I've come across have been the various layers of myself. My work and the people I've met have been my greatest education as to how to reach where I know I'm destined to be.

Keep it simple, my friends. The amount of things Project Woman has been and gone through, I realise most of them were the emotional needs of myself, which led to disappointment because it wasn't about my clients' needs. One of the greatest pieces of advice I can give is don't think you have to do it on your own. That makes it really hard work. Join a network that really supports you, and invites you to offer workshops and talks to build your voice and brand.

Quite simply, if I had the chance to do it all over again, I wouldn't change a thing, because I'm exactly where I'm meant to be right now. Through all the trials, tribulations and adventures, I've come to love myself on the deepest level possible. That means everything. More so to my children, who get to have all of me, instead of just some parts that are appropriate.

The greatest quote I've ever had said to me is by the musician Tom Waits: 'The way you do anything is the way you do everything.' This empowers my relationship not only with my work but also with the deepest part of myself and my family. When I do something, I want to make sure I do it well; so if I'm at a point in my cycle where energy is low, why am I going to do something that requires high energy for a lesser outcome?

This life really is the most magical moment of adventure, excitement and creativity. I shall go to my grave continuing these threads of opportunity, where I invite all to join me.

Big love,

Abi x
www.abiadams.co.uk

EIGHT
Prepare To Leap

It is worth having a defined timeline before you leap from your job. Somewhere you can always easily refer to it – maybe your project notebook or spreadsheet – write down today's date as your starting point. Next, work out a realistic date to quit your job, and add that date to your notes. This span of dates is now your defined timeline. Maintaining your exit date as a focal point will guide you in being more deliberate about allocating your time, energy and finances.

Your timeline is personal to you. There may be some big events that influence your timeline, for example, having a child, a death in the family, the sale of a property, a bonus payout or surgery. Having a gradual, longer-term plan can be useful if you need time to put things into play.

What you can take from your current job

On becoming self-employed, you might stand to lose benefits that came with your job, including private health care, a car allowance or company car, travel insurance, income insurance, life assurance, pension, sick pay, paid holidays, mobile phone insurance. Don't despair – many of these benefits will be tax-deductible from your own business.

It's worth getting a reputable and highly recommended accountant who can advise you appropriately on matters like this. Ask self-employed friends and family members for recommendations on which insurance firms and accountants offer not just the best rates but also the best terms.

Before you escape, you may be able to take advantage of some of the benefits and options you have with your current employer. Here are some examples.

Flexible working

Perhaps, like Laura in the previous chapter, you may be in the fortunate position of being able to reduce your working days by minimising your outgoings, allowing you more time to invest in your career change. As a UK employee, you have the legal right to make a request for flexible working. These requests will not be automatically approved, but employers are required to consider any requests and provide a reason before rejection.

Laura's firm was looking at reducing overheads, so her request for a four-day week was granted. Reducing your salary may not be an option for you, but perhaps you could use flexible working to mitigate commuting costs, for example, by working remotely or travelling outside of peak times.

Selling annual leave

As part of your benefits package, you might be able to sell back unused annual leave entitlement at the end of your annual leave year, which will provide some additional income for when you leap.

Bonuses

If you receive an annual bonus, it's worth checking your contract to make sure you don't resign until after it has been paid. Companies usually stipulate in their employment contracts that you will forfeit your bonus if you resign before the bonus is paid out. Read the fine print of your contract before announcing your departure.

Tax savings

In the UK you can currently contribute up to £60,000 of your salary to your employer's pension fund. You might not be in a position to make sizeable pension contributions, especially if you are trying to build a buffer to escape, but it is worth considering this option. Often, people following the FIRE movement will not only take advantage of the annual £20,000 tax-free saving allowance, but they will also reduce their income tax bill by living frugally and contributing large amounts of their salary into their company pension fund. Some pension schemes allow you to contribute bonuses tax-free straight into your pension fund. This gives a significant advantage, especially if your bonus would otherwise elevate you into a higher tax bracket.

Private medical cover

If you receive private health care from your employer, before you take the leap, have that health assessment you have been putting off. Some private medical policies allow for various treatments, including dental work, eye surgery and holistic therapies. If you have an ailment that needs addressing, it's worth using your employer's medical scheme before jumping ship. In the UK, if you work with computer screens, your employer is obligated to pay for eyesight tests and to make a contribution towards new lenses or glasses.

Job shadowing

This can be useful if you are venturing into a new industry. For example, if you're quitting your city job to create a homestead in the countryside, it is worth spending time on farms, job shadowing to gain skills and learn about the business.

Reskilling

Some employers use external coaching platforms such as BetterUp, which means you might be able to get free coaching. Most companies will have internal training courses or access to, say, LinkedIn Learning, which you might be able to use to upskill. Perhaps your company allows unpaid sabbaticals or secondments to another department where you could upskill.

If your company has a training budget per person, you might be able to use that towards a course relating to your new business. Read the fine print carefully, though, as you may find yourself tied to clawback, meaning you would need to repay the training costs if you resigned within a set period.

Employee assistance

Some companies subscribe to employee assistance programmes, which provide access to third-party legal and financial advice. This can include help with will writing, debt management and family-related counselling matters.

Maternity leave

It is not unusual for women to start a new business when on maternity leave. If you are thinking about starting a family and your firm offers a generous maternity package, you could use this time to test your side hustle.

Jess Munday told *The Sun* that she created Custom Neon while on maternity leave, in response to not being able to find a neon light for her son's nursery. Within five years, she was turning over £9 million and had 32 members of staff.

How to build an audience

Before you take the leap, it is vital to start thinking ahead and building a potential client base. First, always check your contract to understand your obligations. Some firms won't allow you to run another business while still employed, although it may still be possible if you're moving into a different industry and therefore won't be in competition with your current employer.

Here are three ideas to help you gain interest in your new venture:

1. **Build a presence:** While you might be contractually prevented from launching your new business, you could start posting on social media about relevant topics. By gaining followers, you start to build an email list and create a community of potential customers. You could also ask your community questions about your potential product or service, and give free webinars or online training in exchange for testimonials or feedback.

2. **Create a portfolio:** Your portfolio showcases your work and is tangible proof of your skills. Make it diverse to show the range of your skills and abilities. This will be a powerful tool when pitching to prospective clients or investors.

3. **Bootstrapping:** In the startup community, the term bootstrapping is used describe budgeting on a shoestring. There is a tendency for people starting a business to run off and spend a lot of money on adverts and a website, but I highly recommend you don't risk blowing your budget. There are plenty of free websites and tools you can try out before you start making financial commitments. Plenty of successful startups do not invest in online or print advertising. Instead, they use social media to post about their business, or rely on word of mouth or joint ventures. Start small, by leveraging your online network. My recommendation would be not to make large financial commitments until you start generating revenue in the region of £10,000 per month.

I spent my final 12 months of corporate employment experimenting with my business idea. I joined networking groups, tested my idea online, did pro bono work and tried various free tools to work out what I needed. Key for me was avoiding using spreadsheets to track various business activities, such as customer leads, monthly expenditure or conversion rates; instead, I found ways to automate processes. I did not invest in expensive technology and would only go by recommendations. I also retained each receipt in a folder, and I recommend you seek advice from a professional on how far back you can claim expenses before registering your company.

Do not register your business until you have customers, as you will still be required to file an annual company assessment form. Also, check the current threshold at which you are required to register your company for VAT. It is not worth registering for VAT before you meet that threshold unless the products and services you are regularly paying for add up to a large amount of VAT, which you would then want to claim back.

Who can help you

Even if you will be the sole founder of your new business, you don't need to go it alone. Collaboration with other businesses can make a significant difference to the success of your own. Here are two angles you can explore:

1. **Seeking strategic partnerships:** Partnerships or joint ventures can be a shortcut to success. Whether a co-marketing venture or a more intricate business agreement, a partnership can help you quickly tap into an existing audience and customer base, and provide additional resources and credibility. Review your network and determine which industries complement your business. For example, if you are in the luxury fashion business, you may want to partner with other industries in the luxury space such as hospitality or travel. Likewise, if you are a fashion stylist, you may want to establish a joint venture with an executive coach for females in leadership who need outfits to suit their busy lives.

2. **Establishing corporate contracts:** As you establish credibility, set your sights on more substantial opportunities. Larger contracts can offer the consistent income required to confidently transition away from your corporate job. Moreover, they provide valuable networking prospects, connecting you with influential leaders in the industry.

Self-care

Self-care is very important, and admittedly, it's an area where I am great at not following my own advice. I know, though, from experience that I am at my best when I consistently get nine hours' sleep, eat healthily and exercise regularly. As soon as I deviate from just one of these, my productivity slips. If I allow myself to slip into watching Netflix each evening, the nights get later, I snack, and before I know it, I am pressing the snooze button in the morning. When I follow a consistent routine, my energy levels are high, I blast through my workload in a third of the time, and I feel more motivated and achieve more. I have clarity of mind and make fewer mistakes and better decisions. I also feel happier.

If you have hit a slump, replace your couch-potato routine with reading a book or doing a course, for example. This will motivate you to get out of the rut, and you will find that eating better and exercising become easier. If you are stuck in front of a computer all day, you stunt your creative juices. When I get up from my desk and go for a walk, I find an idea or solution comes to me before I return home.

Self-care is different for everyone. For me, the ideal is to book a day off and go to a day spa for a massage, sit in the steam room and have time floating around in the pool. Phones and laptops aren't permitted, so I am forced to switch off and relax.

You're going to be busy, but time out to recharge is crucial, especially if you are running a business. Make sure you carve out time for family and friends too – this time is sacred. Remember, all work and no play makes Jack a dull boy.

Beginning with the end in mind

Now it's time to pull your new future together. There's one final exercise to do.

EXERCISE: Mission statement

A mission statement is a declaration that articulates your career objectives and goals.

Summarise your new career in a concise mission statement. This should be a clear and compelling description of the career you aspire to. It should outline your purpose and direction for your professional journey and can help you clarify your career goals and align your actions with your values and ambitions.

Your mission statement should be SMART to help you remain focused and to track your progress towards achieving your goals.

You should regularly review this statement to ensure it remains aligned to your evolving objectives and aspirations.

Include the following in your mission statement:

- The industry you want to work in
- The career you aspire to have
- Your values that guide your career decisions
- The impact you want to make

Embarking on your career change requires careful planning and strategic decision making. Establishing a clear timeline provides a roadmap for your transition, allowing you to set realistic goals and milestones. Whether you're saving up for a buffer or taking advantage of flexible working arrangements, for example, having a timeline helps to keep you accountable and focused on your objectives. The safety net of your current job allows you to build up your freedom fund and gives you the opportunity to test your minimum viable proposition to see if your business idea has legs before quitting your job. You have the opportunity to experiment with ideas and pivot quickly should an idea not work.

Your mission statement encapsulates your career aspirations and serves as a guiding light throughout your journey. By articulating your industry, career goals, values and desired impact, you align your actions with your vision and remain focused on achieving your objectives.

As you reflect on your progress from the beginning of this book, remember that every step you take will bring you closer to realising your new future. With careful planning and perseverance, and with a clear sense of purpose, you are equipped to navigate the challenges and opportunities that lie ahead on your path to success.

Summary

This chapter has covered the period when you're still in your old job but have a firm timeline for leaving. I have outlined the benefits you can take advantage of before you leave your current employment and the steps you can take towards your new venture while still under contract. Building strategic partnerships at this stage can help get you off to a good start. Finally, your new mission statement will act as your guiding light as you embark on your new venture.

The Maverick Letters

Katie Merrien, CommuniKate Design Limited

Dear (future) founder,

I'm so excited that you're here. Setting out to work for yourself is such an exciting, scary, rewarding and joyful adventure! It also requires a lot of cups of tea.

My visual communications business (CommuniKate Design – because I'm Katie, and I love puns) started through a combination of curiosity, sought opportunities and redundancy. Despite a total lack of business plan, I'm now four and a half years in, and I went fully self-employed one and a half years ago. I still have daily moments of wondering how I get paid to do something I taught myself (I call some of my animations 'Sesame Street style'), and I am so grateful to be here.

I was in my late twenties before I realised you could have a job you actually enjoyed. After skipping university because I couldn't decide what I wanted to study (my original plan of fashion design seems laughable now, given that I usually work in my pyjamas), a temporary office job led to a 13-year career in public sector governance and programme management, which I was good at but didn't enjoy.

Then some of my friends began working at design agencies with table football and beanbags. Their jobs sounded much more fun than mine, but I didn't have any creative experience, so I decided to find ways to be creative in my existing role, by volunteering for as many (vaguely) creative projects as I could.

At the time, I was working to improve services at a GP surgery and needed a way to present the outcomes. I decided to try making an infographic poster on Canva, which later went to a national conference. I also learned how to redesign the surgery's website to make it easier for patients to find the information they needed.

My boss then showed me a graphic recording he'd seen done at an event. I loved it so much I started doodling visual notes (for myself) at meetings and events. Then the new project I was managing decided they needed some animated training videos for the learning modules, so I got a *two-week animation-software free trial and made a practice one. They loved it, so I made more.*

Then I was made redundant.

I accepted a new part-time job to cover my bills, hoping to find extra work with a creative agency at an upcoming recruitment event. Several agencies loved my (animated) CV but explained they didn't have part-time roles.

I realised if I wanted to do creative work, I had to become a freelancer. A freelance what, though? I reflected on the work I'd done and found a common thread: simplifying information to make it accessible. An idea grew for a business that made messages more inclusive by removing complex words – something I'd championed when rewriting NHS websites and patient letters – and turning them into pictures. I came up with a name and strapline ('Making rocket science child's play'), drew a rocket logo and built a website (with some pointers from an IT-whizz colleague). Since then, I've learned and grown through trial and error, luck and hard work. I've shared some of my learning below in the hope it may help you too:

- ***Be curious:** Experiment and try new things. You never know what you'll discover you can do, and what you might be able to transform into a business. Accept you won't be perfect – you'll learn as you grow.*

- ***Find your passion:** Think broadly about what you enjoy and what you're good at. Your offer might not fit a traditional job title, and that's OK. When you* *find the thing(s) you truly love, it doesn't feel like work. Keep checking in with your values too – since I started, I've identified my passion for representing marginalised groups, and I now emphasise that in my offers.*

- **Use resources:** *Business and Intellectual Property Centres (BIPCs) offer free support, resources and one-to-ones to freelancers and small businesses. I only found mine this year, but it's helped me phenomenally. Talk to fellow freelancers too – most will happily share their knowledge with you.*

- **Start slow:** *Starting as a side hustle lets you learn how things work and stay financially secure. Worrying about bills will crush your creativity, so build your client base and leap at the right time (ideally with some savings too).*

- **Use your network:** *Tell everyone, including old colleagues, about your new gig. They know you and your work ethic, and they might welcome your services. Most of my work has come through ex-colleagues and their recommendations.*

- **Know your worth:** *Do market research and price yourself competitively from the start. I started much too low (hello, imposter syndrome!) so people assumed I wasn't skilled. It's easier to set higher prices than renegotiate with clients later.*

- **Don't overstretch:** *Set reasonable goals and prioritise to-do lists (I use Trello). Push yourself, but be cautious about work beyond your scope – saying 'yes' to things* *that you don't know (because you're flattered) leads to tearful late nights and feeling like a failure (you're not; it's just not your area). Be honest about what you offer and respond to requests outlining which part(s) you can do.*

- *Be visible: Networking can feel scary, but there are lots of networking options. Find one that works for you and connect again afterwards on social media. Be yourself in person and online; people buy from people, not businesses.*

- *Get feedback: Collect and share feedback for every project and client. Online reviews are brilliant (free) adverts and help squash imposter syndrome.*

- *Boring bits: Running a business is more than the parts you enjoy. Do the 'boring' bits on days you're less motivated and save fun stuff for days you're excited about work.*

Finally, celebrate your achievements. Creating a sustainable business aligned with your values is amazing, and making any amount of money through your own efforts is incredible.

I know you're going to crush it!

Love,

Katie
https://communikate.design

Conclusion

I hope the stories in this book have not only inspired you but also provided reassurance that another way is possible. That, outside of the corporate cubicle, there is a more creative, wholesome and authentic way to live. Let each one of the stories shared by the incredible beings in this book show you that the leap to that new life is achievable. Each of those people has had doubts and fears and faced their own personal challenges, but in the face of adversity, they have embraced taking action to carve out a life less ordinary and are now enjoying a more meaningful and exciting journey. They wake up each day doing what they love. Despite the detours and challenges they have faced, not one of them regrets their decision. They are all living life on their terms.

I've given you the tools you need to join them, to harness your Fire Power and plan your great leap forward.

Here's to creating something from nothing, embracing the change that comes with starting your own gig, and finding the role you were born to play. This isn't just about a job change – it's also about being the authentic you. As you leap onto this wild ride, remember:

- Your dreams are the roadmap.

- Any setbacks are rich learning detours.

- Every challenge is a chance to grow.

Don't measure your success by comparing yourself with others. You are unique, and this is your journey. Give yourself permission to fly.

Now, go rock that world – I know you can do it.

Please connect with me. I would love to know how your journey is progressing and celebrate your successes, while not overlooking your failures because they are all part of the journey. If you found my book insightful, please drop me a note and tell me about the action you have taken. If you would like clarity on your career change or are looking to bulletproof your job-search process to stand out from the crowd, then head over to www.rozalynwillocks.com or www.linkedin.com/in/get-your-career-unstuck -with-rozalyn and check out my Fire Power Method™ which is a five-step approach to getting unstuck.

Bibliography

Allas, T, 'More UK employees are leaving their jobs than ever before: How businesses can respond' (McKinsey & Company, 26 April 2022), www.mckinsey.com/uk/our-insights/the-mckinsey-uk-blog/more-uk-employees-are-leaving-their-jobs-than-ever-how-businesses-can-respond, accessed 9 February 2024

Aviva, *How We Live: Executive report* (November 2021)

Baker, S, 'Mother-of-three who quit a corporate job making toys to pursue a career as a sculptor reveals she's "found her freedom" and makes artwork from casts of her bottom as an act of rebellion', *Daily Mail* (24 October 2020), www.dailymail.co.uk/femail/article-8863035/Mother-quit-corporate-job-pursue-art-selected-Saatchi-Gallery-exhibit-START-art-fair.html, accessed 27 September 2023

Bartlett, S, 'The diary of a CEO – Karren Brady: How to win at entrepreneurship and love (at the same time)'

(Podchaser, 2022), www.podchaser.com/podcasts/
the-diary-of-a-ceo-with-steven-1021523/episodes/
e133-karren-brady-how-to-win-a-133403156, accessed 29
September 2024

Bergland, C, 'Having social bonds is the no. 1 way to optimize
your health', *Psychology Today* (14 January 2016), www.
psychologytoday.com/gb/blog/the-athletes-way/201601/
having-social-bonds-is-the-no-1-way-optimize-your-health,
accessed 22 February 2024

BBC News, 'The cat who hitched a lift on a worldwide tour', *BBC
News* (29 September 2020), www.bbc.co.uk/news/uk-scotland-
edinburgh-east-fife-54329606, accessed 20 September 2023

Britannica, 'McDonald's: American corporation' (last updated
29 February 2024), www.britannica.com/topic/McDonalds,
accessed 27 February 2024

Canfield, J, *The Success Principles: How to get from where you are to
where you want to be* (HarperCollins, 2005)

Carroll, L and Schrodt, P, 'Why Gen X isn't ready to
leave the workforce', *BBC Worklife* (28 April 2021),
www.bbc.com/worklife/article/20230424-why-gen-x
-isnt-ready-to-leave-the-workforce, accessed 20 September 2023

Chamine, S, 'Know your inner saboteurs' (YouTube, uploaded by
TEDx Talks, 2013), www.youtube.com/watch?v=-zdJ1ubvoXs,
accessed 28 February 2024

Clason, G, *The Richest Man in Babylon* (BN Publishing, 2010)

Economic Times Magazine, 'From an impoverished single mom
to world's richest writer, a look at JK Rowling's incredible
journey' (31 July 2023), https://economictimes.indiatimes.
com/magazines/panache/from-an-impoverished-single
-mom-to-worlds-richest-writer-a-look-at-jk-rowlings-
incredible-journey/when-harry-potter-was-rejected-by-12-
publishers/slideshow/102276515.cms, accessed 22 February 2024

Ferriss, T, *The 4-Hour Work Week: Escape the 9–5, live anywhere and join the new rich* (Crown Publishers, 2007)

Financial Times, 'Cath Kidston sold to Baring Asia' (3 October 2016), www.ft.com/content/8b8ab436-8965-11e6-8cb7-e7ada1d123b1, accessed 23 February 2024

Flade, P, Asplund, J and Elliot, G, 'Employees who use their strengths outperform those who don't' (Gallup, 8 October 2015), www.gallup.com/workplace/236561/employees-strengths-outperform-don.aspx, accessed 29 February 2024

Gallup, 'Employee burnout: Causes and cures' (2 August 2023), www.gallup.com/workplace/508898/employee-burnout-causes-cures.aspx, accessed 27 February 2024

Godin, S, 'Seth Godin: Quieting the lizard brain' (YouTube, uploaded by TEDx Talks, 2015), www.youtube.com/watch?v=qtZfTpV4KPE, accessed 20 November 2023

Hendricks, G, *The Big Leap: Conquer Your Hidden Fear and Take Life to the Next Level* (HarperCollins, 2009)

Hendricks, B, Howell, T and Bingham, C, 'Research: How long should a founder remain CEO?', *Harvard Business Review* (17 December 2021), https://hbr.org/2021/12/research-how-long-should-a-founder-remain-ceo, accessed 20 November 2023

Hinton, J, 'The top six reasons small businesses fail – and how you can avoid them!' (UKBM, 27 June 2023), www.ukbusinessmentoring.co.uk/news/why-do-businesses-fail, accessed 2 March 2024

Kiyosaki, R, *Rich Dad Poor Dad: What the rich teach their kids about money that the poor and middle class do not!* (Plata Publishing LLC, 1997)

Lincoln, K, 'Samuel L Jackson is the highest-grossing actor of all time, according to *The Guinness Book Of World Records*', *Business Insider* (27 October 2011),

www.businessinsider.com/samuel-l-jackson-highest
-grossing-actor-of-all-time-guinness-book-2011-10, accessed 21
October 2023

LinkedIn Pressroom, 'Our skills-first vision for the future'
(29 March 2022), https://news.linkedin.com/2022/march/
our-skills-first-vision-for-the-future, accessed 14 October 2023

LinkedIn Talent Solutions, *The Future of Recruiting* (2024), https://
business.linkedin.com/talent-solutions/resources/future-of-
recruiting?trk=bl-po&veh=FoR_Launch_Post#skills-first-hiring,
accessed 17 March 2024

London School of Business and Finance, 'LSBF survey finds
nearly 50% of UK workers want to change careers' (18 September
2015), www.lsbf.org.uk/blog/opinion-features/lsbf-survey
-finds-nearly-50-of-uk-workers-want-to-change-careers, accessed
21 February 2024

O'Brien, S, 'Generation X carries the most credit card debt,
study shows: Here's how to get those balances down', CNBC
(23 January 2023), www.cnbc.com/2023/01/23/generation-x
-carries-the-most-credit-card-debt-study-shows.html, accessed 23
February 2024

Phoenix Insights, 'Careers advice for longer lives' (Phoenix,
1 May 2023), www.thephoenixgroup.com/phoenix-insights/
publications/careers-advice-longer-lives, accessed 4 March 2024

Ro, C, 'Why the "sandwich generation" is so stressed out',
BBC Worklife (29 January 2021), www.bbc.com/worklife/artic
le/20210128-why-the-sandwich-generation-is-so-stressed-out,
accessed 23 February 2024

Robbins, T, 'How to cultivate a growth mindset' (tonyrobbins.
com, 2024), www.tonyrobbins.com/business/growth-mindset,
accessed 22 November 2023

Robinson, M, 'Tim Ferriss: "You are the average of the five people you most associate with"', *Business Insider* (11 January 2017), www.businessinsider.com/tim-ferriss-average-of-five-people-2017-1, accessed 2 November 2023

Sherif, A, 'Skills on the rise worldwide 2023–2027' (Statista, 4 September 2023), www.statista.com/statistics/1383183/skills-on-the-rise, accessed 9 February 2024

Ware, B, 'Regrets of the dying', https://bronnieware.com/blog/regrets-of-the-dying, accessed 27 February 2024

Wilson, A, 'I started my side hustle with £250 during maternity leave… it now rakes in £9 million a year and I have 32 members of staff', *The Sun* (23 March 2023), www.thesun.co.uk/fabulous/21788934/side-hustle-maternity-leave-9-million-year, accessed 3 March 2024

Further Reading

Articles

Barnicoat, B and Broughton, C, 'What is it like to quit your life and start again?', *The Guardian* (12 June 2024), www.theguardian.com/lifeandstyle/2015/jun/12/five-professionals-give-it-all-to-start-a-new-career, accessed 11 October 2023

Barnicoat, B and Broughton, C, 'UK state pension age will soon need to rise to 71, say experts', *The Guardian* (5 February 2024), www.theguardian.com/money/2024/feb/05/uk-state-pension-age-will-soon-need-to-rise-to-71-say-experts, accessed 13 February 2024

Corfe, O, 'Cost of living over the decades: What life looked like in the 70s, 80s and beyond', *Express*

(4 June 2023), www.express.co.uk/news/
uk/1776789/cost-of-living-over-time-compared-spt,
accessed 13 February 2024

Cox, J, 'How workers are re-defining professional
ambition', *BBC Worklife* (9 September 2021), www.
bbc.com/worklife/article/20210906-are-we-becomin
g-less-ambitious, accessed 29 September 2023

Elliott, K, 'Woman shares "real game changer" after
she transformed £20 kit into £100,000 turnover',
Express (23 January 2023), www.express.co.uk/
finance/personalfinance/1723964/money-making-
tips-resin-side-hustle-uk, accessed 5 October 2023

Evans, R, 'Retirement and me: "Possible for anyone!"
Couple explain how they retired at 35 and 40',
Express (19 June 2022), www.express.co.uk/finance/
personalfinance/1625157/retirement-and-me-
financial-independence-retire-early-FIRE-money-
investing-UK-exclusive, accessed 11 October 2023

Furr, N, 'How failure taught Edison to repeatedly
innovate', *Forbes* (9 June 2011), www.forbes.
com/sites/nathanfurr/2011/06/09/how-failure
-taught-edison-to-repeatedly-innovate, accessed 14
February 2024

Jones, H, 'Meet the people trying to save enough to
retire by 40', *The Guardian* (18 August 2019), www.
theguardian.com/money/2019/aug/18/meet-peopl
e-saving-retire-by-40-fire-movement, accessed 2
March 2024

MyStylist London, 'Mays Al-Ali' (4 September 2019), https://mystylistlondon.co.uk/blogs/inspiring-women/mays-al-ali, accessed 12 October 2023

Nolan, B, 'Workers are "career cushioning" by creating a plan B ahead of a looming recession and sweeping layoffs: Here's how it could protect you', *Business Insider* (4 February 2023), www.businessinsider.com/career-cushioning-recession-layoffs-protect-job-2022-12?r=US&IR=T, accessed 27 February 2024

Ramskill, N, 'Money blocks: How limiting beliefs are keeping you broke' (The Female Money Doctor, 19 December 2019), https://thefemalemoneydoctor.com/money-blocks, accessed 20 January 2020

Scott, E, 'Couple ditch jobs and retire in their 30s to live on a Greek island for £5,000 a year', *Metro* (7 March 2020), https://metro.co.uk/2020/03/07/couple-ditch-jobs-retire-30s-live-greek-island-5000-year-12362827, accessed 11 October 2023

Slater, S, 'Cork woman and London partner are the new caretakers of Great Blasket Island', *Irish Mirror* (10 April 2023), www.irishmirror.ie/news/irish-news/cork-woman-london-partner-new-29673645, accessed 11 October 2023

Stafford, HM-Y, 'Couple quit the rat race and take £125k pay cut to travel the UK in a canal boat', *The Mirror* (23 February 2023), www.mirror.co.uk/travel/uk-ireland/couple-quit-rat-race-take-29295342, accessed 13 October 2023

Thornhill, J and Howard, L (eds), 'Average UK salary by age in 2024', *Forbes* (13 February 2024), www.forbes.com/uk/advisor/business/average-uk-salary-by-age, accessed 13 February 2024

Books

Canfield, J, *The Success Principles: How to get from where you are to where you want to be* (HarperCollins, 2015)

Escape the City Ltd, *The Escape Manifesto: Quit your corporate job: do something different!* (Capstone, 2013)

Stanley, TJ and Danko, WD, *The Millionaire Next Door: The surprising secrets of America's wealthy* (Pocket Books, 1996)

Ware, B, *The Top Five Regrets of the Dying: A life transformed by the dearly departing* (Hay House UK, 2019)

Further Resources

www.bl.uk/bipc
Support for small business owners, entrepreneurs
and inventors

www.britishchambers.org.uk
Independent business network

www.efttrainingcourses.net
Information and courses on EFT

www.enterprisenation.com
Support in starting and growing a business

www.escapethecity.org
Listings for purpose-driven jobs

www.gov.uk/state-pension-age
Information on the state pension age in the UK

www.lepnetwork.net/local-growth-hub-contact
Support for collaborative partnerships

www.macrotrends.net
Research platform for long-term investors

www.statista.com/statistics/1040159/life-expectanc
y-united-kingdom-all-time
Statistics on life expectancy in the UK

www.virginstartup.org
Support for business founders

www.weareumi.co.uk/what-we-do
Business information, advice and support

Acknowledgements

Special thanks to my friend, Maria Broomfield, for always believing in my harebrained schemes, and willing me to keep going and never give up.

To my darling Macintyre, you are the reason I get up each day, especially at 5am! I love you; thank you for keeping me grounded.

To my unofficial godmother, Patty Kuhn, thank you for your faith in me. I take comfort that you are watching over me; I miss you.

I would like to thank the Mavericks featured in the book for trusting me to share their inspirational stories, I'm honoured that you agreed to be part of this journey with me. Adam Moseley, Abi Adams, André

Gagiano, Anja Poehlmann, Chris Bone, Christian Amys, Josh Heyneke, Karen Webber, Katie Merrien, Kieran McMahon, Lara Sheldrake and Ruth Ramsay.

To Sai Blackbryn, thank you for encouraging me to start writing.

To my writing coach, Stephanie Chivers, thank you for being the voice of reason and keeping me on track through the writing process, even when I hit a writing block.

To my mentors, Shaa Wasmund and Matt Thomas, thank you for your guidance.

Thank you to my beta readers, Natalia Pepper and Shelly Groom, for your honest feedback. Thanks too to the incredible female founders in the Found & Flourish community for responding to my questions and cheering me on.

A special thanks to my writing squad, Sarah Manley, Narinder Sheena and Emma Cantrell; and to my best-selling author mentor, Ruth Kudzi, for providing her wisdom.

Finally, thank you to the team at Rethink Press who helped to bring this book to life in a meaningful structure.

The Author

Rozalyn Willocks is a career strategist with a wealth of experience in recruitment, coaching and mentoring. With more than two decades of experience in recruitment, across diverse industries, she is the driving force behind her coaching and mentoring business, Rozalyn Willocks Coaching, and the podcast *Career Mavericks*.

Rozalyn offers her expertise in simplifying the job-search and career change process by using her own Fire Power Method™ developed to help people get unstuck from their present state and take action to reach their desired state. She has honed her expertise and holds certifications from the International Coaching Federation (ICF), in neurolinguistic programming (NLP) and emotional freedom techniques (EFT). She also has a master's in human resource management, and she is passionate about positive intelligence.

As a respected guest on panels and podcasts, and a mentor at the University of Westminster, Rozalyn has had the pleasure of coaching and mentoring hundreds of clients. She thrives on seeing the positive impact the Fire Power Method™ has not only on her clients' careers, but also on their lives. She is passionate about empowering people to realise their potential, be intentional and redefine success.

She exited the rat race in 2011. In 2019 she traded the bustle of London for the serenity of the West Sussex coast, together with her tabby cat, Macintyre, named in homage to the iconic British comedian, Michael Macintyre.

Embracing her inner maverick and unconventional approach, Rozalyn epitomises authenticity. Discover her transformative insights within these pages and embark on a journey of professional self-discovery and growth.

You can find out more about her work here:

- ⊕ www.rozalynwillocks.com
- ▤ www.linkedin.com/in/get-your-career-unstuck -with-rozalyn